A 30-DAY JOURNEY

SHARING GOD'S HEART

by Life in Messiah Staff and Board

LIFE IN MESSIAH

A Resource from Life in Messiah

ISBN: 978-1-878678-09-6

COPYRIGHT
@ 2023 Life in Messiah International
Lansing, IL
www.LifeinMessiah.org

Published in the United States of America

Scripture quotations taken from the (NASB®) New American Standard Bible®, Copyright © 2020 by The Lockman Foundation. Used by permission. All rights reserved. lockman.org.

Scripture quotations marked (AMP) are taken from the Amplified Bible, Copyright © 2015 by The Lockman Foundation. Used by permission.

CONTENTS

Introduction	5
Day 1 – The Measure of Love	7
Day 2 – Can We Talk about an Ish-ue?	11
Day 3 – Adopting God's Views	17
Day 4 – Aligning with God's Heart	25
Day 5 – A Burden Lifted	31
Day 6 – Did That Accomplish Anything?	35
Day 7 – God's Great Distinction	39
Day 8 – Misinformed about Messiah	45
Day 9 – Ancient Words, Ageless Application	49
Day 10 – Beyond Bystanders	53
Day 11 – Casting Away	57
Day 12 – Kill the Carrot	61
Day 13 – To Be Satisfied	65
Day 14 – The God Who Sees	69
Day 15 – Tasting God	75

Day 16 – The Remark	79
Day 17 – A Great Gift from Small Faith	85
Day 18 – "My Rabbi Told Me Not To"	89
Day 19 – Fear of the Known	93
Day 20 – The Language of Truth	97
Day 21 – Provoked to Jealousy	101
Day 22 – Planting Seeds, Tilling Soil	105
Day 23 – Who's Really Converting?	109
Day 24 – Advice for the Doctor	113
Day 25 – An Unexpected Blessing	117
Day 26 – Grieving on Purpose	121
Day 27 – Discovering Passover	125
Day 28 – A Divine Encounter	131
Day 29 – The Slippery Slope of Spiritual Merit	135
Day 30 – Why Jewish Ministry?	141
Keep Learning	147

INTRODUCTION

"Sharing God's heart for the Jewish people." This has been the focus of the ministry of Life in Messiah since our founding in 1887. There are multiple aspects of what sharing God's heart entails. Of course, sharing the gospel with the Jewish people is central to our purpose! God clearly places a priority on the gospel going to the lost and dying world around us. But we also seek to show the love of Messiah to our Jewish friends in meaningful and practical ways.

In addition to sharing the gospel, we intentionally seek out churches and individual believers to educate and equip them to better love the Jewish people in their communities. We emphasize the importance of sharing God's heart for the Jewish people.

It is our desire that we, as believers, would become more and more like our Savior, learning to love whom He loves – which includes the Jewish people.

This book, designed as a 30-day guided reflection on what it means to share God's heart for the Jewish people, is a compilation of articles written by Life in Messiah staff, board members, and partners. These laborers have poured their hearts and ministry experience into these daily readings. Our hope and prayer is that their reflections and stories will be an encouragement to you and a tool for equipping you to proclaim the Good News to the Jewish people in your life.

As Romans 1:16 says: "...I am not ashamed of the gospel, for it is the power of God for salvation to everyone who believes, to the Jew first and also to the Greek."

May you be blessed as you spend the next 30 days reading and meditating on what it means to share God's heart.

Levi Hazen

Levi Hazen, Life in Messiah Executive Director

Day 1

The Measure of Love

*I have loved you with an everlasting love;
Therefore I have drawn you out with kindness.
Jeremiah 31:3b*

"How much do you love me?" is a question humans strive to answer in poetry and prose.

"Wide as the ocean, deep as the seas."

"To the moon and back."

"Many waters cannot quench love, neither can floods drown it," declared Solomon (Song of Solomon 8:7).

"I have loved you with an everlasting love" makes a nice wall plaque – especially meaningful when the author is God.

In Jeremiah 31:3 God is speaking to the Jewish people. And His love for Israel is not a new concept to Bible students.

In the Torah, God states to the Hebrew people, "The LORD did not make you His beloved nor choose you because you were greater in number than any of the peoples, since you were the fewest of all peoples, but because the LORD loved you..." (Deuteronomy 7:7–8a).

But God does more than proclaim His love. He continues, "and kept the oath which He swore to your forefathers, the LORD brought you out by a mighty hand and redeemed you from the house of slavery, from the hand of Pharaoh king of Egypt" (Deuteronomy 7:8b).

It is out of His heart full of love that God acts.

This is not news to Christians. The most-quoted verse of Scripture begins, "For God so loved the world, that He gave His only Son..." (John 3:16a).

Gentile believers in Jesus have reason to revel in the love God has extended to us. As Paul notes, Gentiles who place their trust in Yeshua, the Messiah of Israel, as their personal Savior can count Abraham as their spiritual father by faith (Romans 4:7–12).

Perhaps Paul had insight into what the ensuing centuries would bring. He admonished Gentile believers (the "wild olive branches" of Romans 11) not to boast against the Jewish "natural branches." There is no place for arrogance in the family of faith.

One of Life in Messiah's core values is also our mission statement: "Sharing God's heart for the Jewish people." Romans 9–11 is a great place to see what that should look like.

Paul begins by sharing his own deep grief over the spiritual plight of his kinsmen. His sorrow is grounded in the fact that what God intended as a relationship based on faith (as was Abraham's – see Genesis 15:6) has been replaced by a religion of works-righteousness and rule-keeping.

In contrast to what many Christian leaders have taught over the centuries, "God has not rejected His people whom He foreknew" (Romans 11:2). Israel's spiritual blindness is both partial and temporary. A glorious spiritual restoration is promised to the Jewish people (Romans 11:25-27).

From God's perspective, even enemies of the gospel remain "beloved on account of the fathers; for the gifts and the calling of God are irrevocable" (Romans 11:28-29).

This is an echo of God's promise back in Jeremiah 31:31 and following. A new covenant will be written on the hearts of God's people (specified as "the house of Israel and the house of Judah"). Sins will be fully forgiven.

The people of Israel are as enduring as are the promises of their God. The fixed order of the heavenly bodies will cease before God forgets His covenant with Jacob's offspring.

Our mission at Life in Messiah is twofold as we share God's heart of love.

First, we speak to the church, reminding Christians of God's steadfast, loyal love for the Jewish people. We tell of the spiritual debt we owe them. And we point to the biblical priority in evangelism.

Second, we seek to demonstrate God's love to our Jewish friends in practical ways. We remind them of God's promises of a redeemer. We share the Scriptures that point to Messiah. And we show how the prophesies were fulfilled in Yeshua, Jesus of Nazareth.

Love: it's more than what makes the world go 'round. It's the motivator of a holy God to redeem sinful mankind.

If we are to fulfill the Great Commandment to "love the Lord with all your heart, and with all your soul, and with all your mind, and with all your strength" (Mark 12:30), we must love what He loves.

And if we are to "love your neighbor as yourself" (Mark 12:31), we will seek the blessing and joy for others that comes from receiving God's greatest gift of love: Yeshua.

Application

Do you love what God loves? Ask God how He wants you to share His heart for the Jewish people.

Day 2

Can We Talk about an Ish-ue?

Let no unwholesome word come out of your mouth, but if there is any good word for edification according to the need of the moment, say that, so that it will give grace to those who hear.
Ephesians 4:29

Can we talk about an ish-ue?

Well-meaning Christians often use the words "Jew" or "Jews" in reference to a Jewish person or the wider Jewish community. After all, "Mordecai the Jew" is found in the Bible; the Gospels and Paul often mention "the Jews."

In seeking to share God's heart for the Jewish people, we often discuss the value of using words that best communicate to our audience. So, why would we make use of "Jews" an issue (*ish-ue*)?

If you think about it, to append *ish* can be really helpful in many circumstances. *Ish* adds descriptive flavor to terms like "boorish" or "stylish."

But we're talking about appending *ish* where it adds more than description; it takes a word to a whole new level.

After all, a dish without *ish* is a lonely D awaiting a vowel and a consonant or two to help make it into something proper.

Yes, the simple addition of *ish* transforms the fourth letter of the alphabet into "dish." Whether it is now a satellite dish, a dog dish, part of a table setting or to be used as a descriptive shape or a wonderful culinary delight, you must agree it is the *ish* that lifts D to such a level.

What is the letter F when standing alone? A negative feeling of failure is associated with F – until you add on those letters *ish*. Suddenly the word swims to life as "fish." Images spring to mind of savory salmon or beautiful coral-reef life. Once again, a letter is lifted by the simple addition of *ish*.

Uplifting, after all, is what Christians aspire to be. Whether in word or deed, we lift up the person who is our Messiah and Savior. We want all humanity to be drawn to Him.

Finally, we come to that letter with the confusing name: W. Yes, it is "double-U" (or is it "double-you"?).

With that wonderful addition of *ish* we see another transformation – from hopeless W to hopeful "wish." Suddenly, aspirations and dreams are in view. Birthday cakes and candles and wishes appear – all with the addition of three letters.

And now we focus on the real *ishue* before us: "Jew" or "Jewish"?

Have you considered that "Jew" might sound different in a Jewish ear when spoken by non-Jewish lips? Truth be told, the term "Jew" on a Christian's lips can sound as jarring as fingernails on a chalkboard to our Jewish friends. "Why so?" you may ask.

Too often in history, the word "Jew" has been said with a sneer or spat out in anger. It is often accompanied by a derogatory adjective: "cheap Jew" or "dirty Jew." "Christ-killing Jew" dredges up images of the Christian Crusades, the Inquisition, or pogroms (organized persecution of Jewish communities).

So when "Jew" is spoken by a Gentile, it can have the effect of sounding an alarm. Emotional walls of protection quickly go up. Ears of receptivity slam shut like a door against an intruder.

On the other hand, "Jewish person" and "Jewish community" elicit a different response in a Jewish ear (note: not "in the ear of a Jew"). As when fabric softener is used to wash a favorite towel, the words not only sound nice but also *feel* nice in our Jewish friends' ears.

Adding *ish* to "Jew" simply sounds more pleasant. "Jewish" recognizes the sensitivity and historical suffering of our Lord's own kindred. The walls built by centuries of antisemitism begin to come down. Rather than pointing a finger of accusation or distaste, we offer a kind hand of understanding. All because of the beauty of *ish*.

So, remember: if as a Christian you want your Jewish friends to listen to what you dish and to realize the love associated with our ancient symbol of the fish, then have the sensitivity and awareness to add the *ish*! This is, well, my wish!

Application

Do you see the value in changing your words to be more sensitive to Jewish people? Offensive words can create avoidable barriers to the gospel. We can demonstrate Jesus' kindness by speaking with sensitivity.

Note:

If the Bible uses the word "Jews," why should we substitute the term "Jewish people"?

First, most of the writers of Scripture were Jewish themselves. Some things, like ethnic jokes, may be acceptable for use within the community – but not by those outside of it. Second, historical and cultural context matters. Word usage and the nuance of their meaning changes over time. Terms that were once acceptable can become distastefully associated with ugly historical events. For example, we don't often hear of a baby named Adolf (because of Adolf Hitler).

So, continue reading God's Word in its context: the gospel is "to the Jew first and also the Greek" (Romans 1:16). But in our conversation with the people chosen and loved by God (Deuteronomy 7:6–8, Jeremiah 31:3), let's add *ish*.

Day 3

Adopting God's Views

For the Lord of armies says this: "After glory He has sent me against the nations that plunder you, for the one who touches you, touches the apple of His eye."
Zechariah 2:8

Does God love everyone? John 3:16 tells us He does.

"Does God love everyone equally?" is another question. God's statement, "Jacob have I loved but Esau I have hated" is a challenge to our sense of fairness – especially when the choice was made while the twins were in utero (Romans 9:10–13). What about "the disciple whom Jesus loved" (John 21:20)?

What does it mean to have God's heart for the Jewish people? Foundationally, it means recognizing their unique role as His chosen people and loving them as He does. For a sampling, Scriptures describe Israel as the apple of God's eye (Zechariah 2:8), His treasured possession (Exodus 19:5, Deuteronomy 14:2), His inheritance (Deuteronomy 4:20), His children (Deuteronomy 14:1), and His wife (Jeremiah 31:32).

The Jewish people are precious in God's sight, honored and loved (Isaiah 43:4), and His witnesses and servant (Isaiah 43:10). God is Israel's Redeemer, "the Holy One of Israel," their Creator and King (Isaiah 43:14–15). He has engraved them on His palms (Isaiah 49:15–15).

The Scriptures are very clear: Israel matters a great deal to God. And the prophetic words which accompany such expressions of love indicate this love is not merely past tense (see Isaiah 43:5–7 as one example in context).

What does love look like? Pastor Steve DeWitt of Bethel Church in Crown Point, Indiana, defines love as "actively seeking the good and joy of others." So how do we seek the good and joy of the Jewish people?

First, we should not overlook the Jewish people's need. Over the years we have noted with sadness how easy it is for the Jewish people not to be represented in missions conferences on college campuses and in churches. We often see specific seminars on reaching Muslims, Hindus, Buddhists, or animists, but many times the Jewish people aren't on the program.

Many evangelical churches work to diversify their missions giving, yet often no Jewish ministry is on the budget. The clear biblical priority of the Jewish people in God's plan has dropped entirely off the radar for many. Our esteemed colleague Jhan Moskowitz (now with the Lord) said it well: "The greatest form of antisemitism is the withholding of the gospel from the Jewish people."

Thankfully, there are wonderful exceptions. Our hearts soar when we hear of messages preached in local churches that reflect God's heart for the Jewish people.

Second, we should recognize Israel's distinctness from the church. Supersessionism is reflected in a theology that reads the church back into the Old Testament and considers Israel to be the church in the New Testament. The failure to distinguish between God's dealings with national Israel and His purpose for the global church produces numerous errors.

As examples, God's unconditional covenant regarding the Land promised to Abraham (Genesis 15) gets spiritualized or ignored. Specific commands to national Israel are confusing when applied to the church. What is the New Covenant believer's relationship to laws about observing the Sabbath, eating unclean foods, or mixing cotton and linen in clothing?

We can love the Jewish people by refusing to spiritualize or misappropriate God's blessings for Israel. "Every promise in the book is mine / every chapter every verse every line" is a catchy song reflecting a lousy hermeneutic, in my opinion.

Third, we should remember God's blueprint for the church. In Ephesians 2:13–16, Paul details God's design for the Bride of Messiah:

> But now in [Messiah] Jesus you [Gentiles] who previously were far away have been brought near by the blood of [Messiah]. For He Himself is our

peace, who made both groups [Jews and Gentiles] into one and broke down the barrier of the dividing wall, by abolishing in His flesh the hostility, which is the Law composed of commandments expressed in ordinances, so that in Himself He might make the two one new person, in this way establishing peace; and that He might reconcile them both in one body to God through the cross, by it having put to death the hostility.

The result of Messiah's work on the cross, for both Jewish and non-Jewish believers in Him, includes peace (verse 17), access in one Spirit to the Father (verse 18), and being built together to be God's dwelling place (verse 22).

Ephesians 3:6 unveils the mystery: "[This mystery is] that the Gentiles are fellow heirs and fellow members of the body, and fellow partakers of the promise in [Messiah] Jesus through the gospel." Hallelujah!

Fourth, let's have an attitude of humble gratitude! As Gentiles, our spiritual heritage was destitute: we were dead in trespasses and sins (Ephesians 2:1–2). But this is true of Jewish people as well. In Paul's words, "For we have already charged that both Jews and Greeks are all under sin; as it is written: 'There is no righteous person, not even one; there is no one who understands, there is no one who seeks out God" (Romans 3:9–11).

However, Scripture contrasts the spiritual legacy of the two groups.

The Jewish inheritance (Romans 9:4–5):

> "[They] are Israelites, to whom belongs the adoption as sons and daughters, the glory, the covenants, the giving of the Law, the temple service, and the promises; whose are the fathers, and from whom is the [Messiah] according to the flesh, who is over all, God blessed forever. Amen."

The Gentile position (Ephesians 2:11–12):

> "Therefore remember that previously you, the Gentiles in the flesh, who are called 'Uncircumcision' by the so-called 'Circumcision' which is performed in the flesh by human hands – remember that you were at that time separate from [Messiah], excluded from the people of Israel, and strangers to the covenants of the promise, having no hope and without God in the world."

One could almost think Paul foresaw what could happen down the road as more Gentiles were added to the Body (and he saw the continuing resistance of his kinsmen to the gospel). Using an olive tree analogy, Paul writes to the non-Jewish "wild branches," instructing them, "Do not be arrogant toward the [natural] branches" (see Romans 11:17–21).

Reading the words of the church fathers regarding the Jewish people, we get the sense that Paul's injunction has been widely ignored. Even understanding the difficulties of discerning motivations and the forces shaping cultures far removed from ours, it is easy to see how Jewish people reading the patristic writings don't come away feeling loved and valued.

After the church was birthed (Acts 2), Gentiles heard the gospel of the Jewish Messiah from Jewish witnesses. Are we grateful?

Finally, let's remind others of God's covenant faithfulness! This can be done by preaching from biblical passages that both teach and illustrate this truth (Ezekiel 20 is my favorite, in part because it is unfamiliar to many.)

But we also have tangential opportunities to reference God's *hesed* (a Hebrew word describing God's steadfast loving-kindness). As one example, when citing A.W. Pink's 17 qualities of God, the first three qualities (uninfluenced, eternal, and sovereign) all are directly related to God's love for the Jewish people. Surely His qualities of love extend to all people. But this would be a great place to remind the church of God's enduring love for the Jewish people, simply by noting the context of the quoted passages. God's covenant steadfastness to Israel bolsters our confidence that He will not forsake us (2 Timothy 2:13 is a New Testament restatement of this wonderful truth).

Application

Based on what you've just read and the Scriptures we've looked at, do you have any views that you need to adjust to match God's? Ask God to work in your heart and mind in these areas.

Day 4

Aligning with God's Heart

Brothers and sisters, my heart's desire and my prayer to God for them is for their salvation.
Romans 10:1

What does love look like? As mentioned in yesterday's reading, Pastor Steve DeWitt defines love as "Actively seeking the good and joy of others." So how do we seek the good and joy of the Jewish people? In today's reading we consider five more suggestions.

First, we should consider national Israel's future. What are the implications of the biblical promises yet unfulfilled? Surely if everything culminated with the church being gathered to her Bridegroom, the glorious Marriage Supper of the Lamb, and the ushering in of the eternal state, God could simply destroy Earth after uniting us to His Son. But Daniel's 70th week (see Daniel 9) picks up where the 69th week leaves off – with Israel in primary focus.

It will be to the Jewish people whom Messiah reveals Himself when His feet touch down on the Mount of Olives (Zechariah 14:3–5) after His wrath and judgments have been poured out on the nations who oppress the Jewish people during the Tribulation. In Zechariah 12:2 and 3, God says He will "make Jerusalem a cup that causes staggering to all the peoples around.... And all the nations of the earth will be gathered against [Jerusalem]."

Zechariah 12:7–9 details the physical deliverance of the Jewish people. But it is verse 10 that makes our hearts thrill: "And I will pour out on the house of David and on the inhabitants of Jerusalem the Spirit of grace and of pleading, so that they will look at Me whom they pierced; and they will mourn for Him, like one mourning for an only son, and they will weep bitterly over Him like the bitter weeping over a firstborn."

Zechariah 13 tells of the fountain opened for cleansing from sin and Israel's spiritual restoration. And then we have the reign of Yeshua (Zechariah 14:9), with Jerusalem the capital. And the Jewish Festival of Booths will be observed – even by Gentiles (Zechariah 14:16–19).

When it comes to their identities, prophetic roles, and the promises given to them, the church and Israel are not identical people of God. Nor are they in competition. Right now, Jewish people and Gentiles are being united through faith in the Body of Messiah – the church. And if we understand correctly, the saints will return to reign with Yeshua when He takes David's throne and begins His earthly reign.

This culminating reign on earth will bring full circle God's prophetic purpose for the physical descendants of Jacob. It will result in God's greater glory among the nations – something repeatedly referenced in the Bible. This matters to God – look how much of Holy Writ is devoted to it. Should it not matter to us?

Second, we must speak the truth in love. Scripture is clear: the Jewish people need the Savior. They (and the church) need to be reminded of this need. The Jewish people (like all others) are under God's judgment.

When we speak of God's wrath over Israel's unbelief and disobedience, we should do so with the sorrow reflective of Jeremiah and Jesus. Our very tone of voice when speaking of the Jewish people communicates much. Do we speak with warmth and tenderness, or with indifference, dismissiveness, or derision?

I once observed a believer who literally backed a stranger into a corner, wagged his finger under the poor trapped man's nose and said angrily, "You're going to burn in hell if you don't repent."

The response came quickly: "And something tells me you'd be happy if I did go to hell." *Oy!*

Third, we need to align our ministry priorities with God's. Most Gentiles are fine with Paul's statement that judgment is "to the Jew first" (Romans 2:8–9).

However, more often than not, Romans 1:16 is quoted incompletely: "For I am not ashamed of the gospel, for it is the power of God for salvation to everyone who believes." But God didn't end there! The full verse says, "For I am not ashamed of the gospel, for it is the power of God for salvation to everyone who believes, *to the Jew first and also to the Greek*" (emphasis ours).

Fourth, we need to understand Jewish sensitivities and culture. Love pays attention to the wants and needs of others in order to maximize their good and joy. The deep wounds the Jewish people have suffered over centuries – too often at the hands of those identified as Christians – is a huge barrier to the gospel.

It seems a minor step, but replacing unfamiliar or historically weighted words with vocabulary that is more friendly or familiar to Jewish ears (e.g., replacing *Christ* with *Messiah*, *Jesus* with *Yeshua*, *Jews* with *Jewish people*, or *Old Testament* with *Hebrew Scriptures*) helps our Jewish friends feel more at home with us.

Jewish holidays provide a great opportunity for building bridges – and for Gentiles to explore the Jewish roots of our faith and gain insights into Scripture. Participating in a Messiah-focused Passover meal is one example (Life in Messiah is delighted when churches invite us to host these). Another idea is for churches to put out a sign with a message like, "Happy New Year to our Jewish friends" during Rosh Hashanah.

Last, we need to get to know the Jewish people around us! It's impossible to love in a vacuum. The best love is what Yeshua (Jesus) modeled: incarnational and relational love. Spending time with Jewish people, listening to their stories and sharing our own, is something anyone can do.

For a conversation starter with a Jewish friend, consider asking for their perspective on Christians, the Christian community, and the history of Christian antisemitism. How wonderful it would be to counter misperceptions of Jesus by contrasting the hateful actions of some with His clear teachings (we are to love even our enemies, etc.) and with acts of loving-kindness toward our Jewish neighbors.

As always, so much more could be said on the topic of loving the Jewish people, but I'll stop here. May God help us – His church – to reflect His love for His chosen nation.

Application

What are some practical ways you can begin showing care to the Jewish people?

Day 5

A Burden Lifted

And He said to him, "You shall love the Lord your God with all your heart, and with all your soul, and with all your mind."
Mathew 22:37

I was in New York City, handing out materials regarding the promised Messiah, when a woman approached me.

"I can't possibly keep the 613 laws in the Torah," she said. "It's too burdensome."

As a newbie in Jewish evangelism, I wasn't quite sure how to respond, but my mouth opened anyways. "You are right, no one can," I began. "But I believe the Messiah has come, and we know He brings a New Covenant. And did you know this covenant has only two commandments?"

The woman's eyes softened and I saw a weight lifted off her shoulders. "Can this really be true?" she asked.

"Absolutely!" I said. "And here is the first commandment: 'Love the Lord your God with all your heart and with all your soul and with all your mind.' And the second one: 'Love your neighbor as yourself'" (see Matthew 22:35–40).

The look on the woman's face was priceless. To see the weight of the Law lifted off her and replaced by a look of hope was beautiful. Soon after, the woman disappeared into the crowd. To this day, I have no idea who she was or if I'll ever see her again. All I know is that she touched my life as I hope I touched hers.

As a Gentile, I have never experienced the full weight of the Law – having to turn down a bacon cheeseburger, ritually cleansing every month, buying my clothes from special stores where they don't mix textiles, fasting on certain days; the list goes on.

The Lord ushered me into a life of freedom and grace, enabling me to leave my sin-cursed life behind and bypassing the blessed Mosaic Law along with its impossibly strict commands.

Thinking of my Jewish friends, seeking to daily uphold 613 laws seems exhausting to say the least. I know the Law is good and sweeter than honey (Psalm 19:7, 9–10; Psalm 119:103), but it was meant only for a time and was designed to point us to the Messiah (Galatians 3:34, Hebrews 7:18–19, Hebrews 10).

Will you join me by sharing this life-giving message with your Jewish friends? We have such great news! News that their yoke will be made easy and their burden light

(Matthew 11:28–30) if they receive Yeshua (Jesus) as their Jewish Messiah.

Application

Is there something preventing you from sharing this burden-lifting message of grace and forgiveness with your neighbor/coworker today? Ask God to give you the courage, understanding, and grace to share the Good News.

Day 6

Did That Accomplish Anything?

*Let's not become discouraged in doing good, for in due time we will reap, if we do not become weary.
Galatians 6:9*

As the clacking train wheels closed the distance between Amsterdam and my home, I looked out at the level green landscape. A small village appeared in the distance and a steeple on a weathered stone church rose from a small cluster of brick homes.

Reviewing our evangelistic outreach of the previous day, I recalled the encounter my friend and I had had with a young man. By his appearance and demeanor, I deduced that he was an Israeli serving as a security guard in the area near a Jewish religious school.

In his native language, Hebrew, I asked him if he wanted a free gift, a Hebrew New Testament. A mix of surprise and caution flooded his face.

My surmise of his occupation proved correct. His trained eyes carefully focused on my right hand as

I reached deep into my shoulder bag to retrieve the book for him. He extended his own hand to receive it.

Did that really accomplish anything? I now pondered from my train seat. I had only handed him a small Bible in his language; no significant conversation had resulted. He'd simply gotten a smile from a stranger, along with a book he hadn't asked for.

Over many years I've had similar encounters with people from numerous cultures in an assortment of countries. Sometimes doubts seep in about the effectiveness of such random and often quick exchanges. Once again, those pinpricks of ambivalence poked my consciousness as the Netherlands' beautiful scenery swept by.

A week or so later, I was walking beside a still canal that cut through our city when suddenly an acquaintance named Morris came to mind. Years earlier, just before a service I was scheduled to speak in, the pastor had introduced me to Morris. A 20-something fellow believer in Jesus, Morris would be sharing after me, describing God's call on his life as an Israeli believer.

During the service, I enthusiastically shared the things the Lord had been allowing me to do: having evangelistic conversations, teaching, and distributing gospel literature. I shortened my presentation to give time for everyone to hear from Morris.

Our Israeli brother smiled as he took the podium. "Jeff, I want to thank you for what you are doing," Morris said. "God used someone just like you to open my eyes, and eventually I came to faith in Yeshua as Messiah.

"My faith journey started three years ago," he continued. "I was in Jerusalem when a man I'd never seen before pressed a book into my hand as he walked past. God used that book about Yeshua as the first step in the journey that brought me to faith in Him as my Messiah!"

This memory reminded me anew: God often uses us despite our sometimes bungling efforts to accomplish His purposes. Our acts of obedience make a difference when God and faith are involved!

Application

Have you been discouraged by a lack of visible fruit from evangelism? Ask God to show you what He can accomplish through your obedience.

Day 7

God's Great Distinction

Do not offend Jews or Greeks, or the church of God; just as I also please everyone in all things, not seeking my own benefit but the benefit of the many, so that they may be saved.
1 Corinthians 10:32–33

Recently I was discussing the Bible's teaching on Israel and the church when my conversation partner said, "After all, we Christians are spiritual Jews."

This was not my first time hearing this statement; it is a belief held by many Christians. Like so many other pithy phrases, many people assume it is true just because it is often repeated and sounds good.

A number of passages have been used to support the idea that Gentile believers are now spiritual Jews. This belief has been taught throughout much of church history and remains prevalent in some seminaries and churches today. But does Scripture actually teach that Gentile believers become spiritual Jews when they believe in Jesus?

Let's address some commonly misunderstood passages by examining them in their context. First, let's consider the question, "Are all of Abraham's descendants Jewish?"

Romans 9:6-7 says, "But it is not as though the word of God has failed. For they are not all Israel who are descended from Israel; nor are they all children because they are Abraham's descendants, but: 'Through Isaac your descendants shall be named.'"

Based on this passage, some teach that since Gentile believers are called "Abraham's descendants," they now compose a "new" or "spiritual Israel."

However, physical or spiritual descent from Abraham alone does not make someone Jewish. Remember that Abraham fathered both Jewish and Gentile lines through his sons Ishmael and Isaac and grandsons Jacob and Esau. But Romans 9:7 specifies that "...Through *Isaac* [Abraham's] descendants shall be named" (emphasis ours). God is clear that only those descended from Abraham *and* Isaac *and* Jacob are Jewish (see Genesis 21:12, 28:13–15; Romans 9:13). Anyone not descended from Abraham, Isaac, and Jacob is a Gentile by default (including Ishmael's and Esau's descendants).

That said, let's be clear: being Jewish or Gentile has no bearing on God's love for us. God loves the world and desires everyone to be saved (John 3:16, 2 Peter 3:9).

A second fallacy that often accompanies the first is the belief that, when the Bible speaks of Israel, it refers to a group consisting of all people who believe in Jesus (Abraham's spiritual descendants) rather than the Jewish people. Are believers really the new Israel?

In Romans 11 Paul teaches that much of Israel remains in unbelief (see Romans 9:31–32 and 11:25–29) and that Israel is experiencing a "partial hardening" (Romans 11:25). Can believers be hardened against salvation and still be saved? Can Gentile believers be Israel in belief while at the same time being Israel in unbelief? This is impossible, of course!

So, what is Paul really teaching in Romans 9:6–7? He is teaching that a "true" Jewish person is one who believes in Israel's Messiah, Jesus. In Romans 9:8–13, he provides a fuller explanation.

Reading beyond the immediate context of verses 6–7, it's clear Paul is not expanding his definition of Jewishness to include believing Gentiles or a "new Israel." Rather, Paul is narrowing his definition of who is truly Jewish. He differentiates between a Jewish person who belongs to Israel by physical decent and one who belongs to Israel by physical decent as well as belief in the Messiah.

As an example, let's say Sam and I are graduates of Taylor University. I am a big fan of Taylor's football team, the Trojans. I attend every home game, possess school memorabilia, and visit campus regularly. I am proud to be identified as a Trojan.

When I ask if Sam is going to the next football game, he tells me he has other plans. In fact, Sam says he has not been to campus in a decade. Sam's lack of interest in the football program and his absence from campus tells me that, although he is a graduate of Taylor University, Sam is not a true Trojan fan. I've narrowed the definition of what it means to be a true Trojan, just as Paul narrows the definition of a true Jew.

A true Jewish person, according to Paul, is one who believes in the Jewish Messiah, Jesus. Yet Paul still unequivocally refers to unbelieving Israel as "Israel" (Romans 11:1–10). He does not teach that Gentiles are now spiritual Jews or that the church comprises a new Israel. In all Paul's writings throughout Scripture, Gentiles remain Gentiles and Jewish people remain Jewish, regardless of their beliefs.

Another commonly misinterpreted verse is Galatians 3:27–29: "For all of you who were baptized into Christ have clothed yourselves with Christ. There is neither Jew nor Greek, there is neither slave nor free, there is neither male nor female; for you are all one in Christ. And if you belong to Christ, then you are Abraham's descendants, heirs according to promise."

I have heard some say, "There is no Jew or Greek in Christ," to argue that Jewish people lose their ethnic identity once they come to faith. Some then wrongly conclude that the church is the "new Israel."

The New Testament uses the word "Israel" 73 times. Not once does it mean the church. Instead, it always refers to either national, ethnic Israel or Jewish believers.*

So what is Galatians 3:27–29 really teaching?

If we look at the verse in context, we see Paul is teaching that each person, regardless of ethnicity, gender, or whether they are enslaved, must come to God through faith in Messiah. Whatever our differences in background, everyone must approach God the same way: believing in Messiah's atoning sacrifice in our place.

Upon trusting in the Messiah, do women stop being women? Do Asians stop being Asian? Of course not! In the same way, Jewish people do not stop being Jewish and Gentiles do not stop being Gentiles. We continue to enjoy and celebrate our God-given differences. God created these distinctions within humanity – including whether one is Jewish or Gentile – for His own glory.

The same concept is true about Israel and the church. The New Testament always makes a distinction between the two, and so should we (see 1 Corinthians 10:32 and Ephesians 2:11–22; Jewish and Gentile believers are united in Messiah's body, the church, but retain their ethnic distinctives)! Just like the distinctions between male and female, the distinctiveness of Israel and the

*Michael J. Vlach, *Has the Church Replaced Israel?* (Nashville: B&H Publishing Group, 2010), 199.

church ultimately brings more glory to God. So, the next time you hear someone teaching that "Christians are spiritual Jews," please remind them of God's great distinction.

Application

What are some dangers that can arise with confusing the church and Israel? What do these passages reveal about the identity of Israel?

Day 8

Misinformed about Messiah

For our exhortation does not come from error or impurity or by way of deceit; but just as we have been approved by God to be entrusted with the gospel, so we speak.
1 Thessalonians 2:3-4a

"That's good," Betty told me. "I think it's really nice that you have a strong faith. But do you know who I don't like? It's those Jews who believe in Jesus!"

I was silent for a moment as I studied my friend, who was herself Jewish. She was sitting in a chair in front of my desk at my property management office. I always enjoyed when Betty stepped into my office for a chat. She was intelligent, witty, caring, and quite direct when speaking about things that really mattered to her.

Yet there was no mistaking the disdain in her voice and the change in her usually serene demeanor as she uttered the words "*those Jews* who believe in Jesus."

I was caught off guard by Betty's remark because she knew I was serious about my faith. In fact, she had spoken with me in the past of her respect for Christians who followed their faith wholeheartedly.

I chose my words carefully. "Betty, do you realize how offensive what you just said is?"

Surprise filled her face and voice. "What? Offensive to *you* that I spoke about Jews?"

"Betty," I responded, "Why do you get so upset with Jewish people who believe in Jesus?"

"Why? Well, because it is wrong for a Jew to worship a man!" Her voice was even louder now.

"Yes, I understand," I replied after a long pause. "And I agree with you one hundred percent, Betty. And that is what is offensive!"

I could see that my answer confused her, so I pressed on. "Yes, it is wrong to worship a man as God. But you seem to believe it is only wrong for *Jewish people*...that it's okay for someone like *me* to 'worship a man.'"

I could see now that Betty had fully realized the implications of her belief. For a few moments there was an uneasy silence.

With a smile, I again looked into Betty's eyes. "I know you wouldn't purposely say something to offend me," I said. "What it really comes down to, Betty, is what I consider the most important question everyone should seek to answer: Who was – or is – Jesus?"

I made sure my tone was warm as I added that I believed that there was only one God, and that He was the God of Israel, our Creator. I shared that God did not want anyone to worship a false god or man, whether Jewish or Gentile. This was the reason, I explained, why the true nature and identity of Jesus is so important.

Then I started to say, "Because if Jesus was the Son of God, then... " when Betty raised a hand to silence me. She smiled faintly as she reached across the desk and gently placed her hand on mine, giving it a slight squeeze. Then she rose from her chair. "I know you mean well," she said.

Those final words – sincere words – were the last ones I ever heard from Betty.

Today, this same old, sad belief permeates the Jewish community and keeps them from "believing" what the Hebrew Scriptures clearly say about God's Son (see Proverbs 30:1–5, Psalm 2, 110:1; Daniel 7:13–14, Matthew 22:41–46), who He is, and how He promised to bring about salvation.

The sad reality is that for centuries, and still today, much misinformation has been proclaimed about the Jewish man who was born in Bethlehem in Israel, just as the prophet Micah prophesied (Micah 5:2). There are many people today (Jewish and Gentile) who think like

Betty. They are victims of misinformation about the Jewish Messiah – Jesus.

Yet there is a trustworthy source: the Hebrew Scriptures (a good starting point is Isaiah 40:9 and Isaiah 52:13–53:12). The Scriptures are trustworthy, informative, and show without manipulation the true identity of the Jewish Messiah.

Application

Have you encountered people who are misinformed about Jesus? What can you do or say to gently redirect them to the truth? Ask God to guide your words as you share the truth about His Son.

Day 9

Ancient Words, Ageless Application

In everything, therefore, treat people the same way you want them to treat you, for this is the Law and the Prophets.
Mathew 7:12

Many within Judaism consider the Golden Rule to be a summarizing commandment of the Torah: "...You shall love your neighbor as yourself; I am the Lord" (Leviticus 19:18).

Many renowned rabbis of the past, such as Rabbi Hillel, Rabbi Akiva, and others, echoed these words and gave their interpretations of their meaning. Hillel the Elder said this: "That which is hateful to you do not do to another; that is the entire Torah, and the rest is its interpretation. Go study" (see Talmud tractate Shabbat 31a:6).

The identity of the "neighbor" and how to understand and apply this verse has been discussed through the centuries. Jesus spoke of this core command when He taught, "'And you shall love the Lord your God with all your heart, and with all your soul, and with all your mind, and with all your strength.' The second is this: 'You shall love your neighbor as yourself.' There is no other commandment greater than these" (Mark 12:30–31).

We need only read headlines from around the world to know that violence, corruption, crushing wars, and needless bloodshed abound. If people would truly embody the Golden Rule, how different our world would look.

Many Jewish people champion what is called *tikkun olam*, a desire to mend or repair the world. In many circles this has become a rallying cry for social justice. But many rabbis bemoan the way *tikkun olam* has morphed into something beyond the term's original intent. Certainly the idea that the Jewish people (or anyone else) can truly fix what is broken in this world excludes the truth that only God can repair His creation.

In his book, *Jewish Giftedness and World Redemption: The Calling of Israel*, author Jim Melnick writes,

> The crucial element missing in most Jewish views of *tikkun olam* is a concern for souls and eternal salvation, whereas this is the very essence of a New Testament view of "doing good deeds." The ultimate goal of the latter is not just to feed the poor and clothe the naked but to share the love of God with others so that some may come to a saving faith in Messiah.

Both the Golden Rule and *tikkun olam* are missing something – or someone.

One day God Himself will repair His physical creation and fulfill His promises to His people Israel. But first, He sent One to repair our souls and our broken relationship with Him. Jesus placed the command to "love your neighbor as yourself" after the command to love God "with all your heart, and with all your soul, and with all your mind, and with all your strength."

The key to succeeding in the Golden Rule is to fulfill the first great command – and therein lies our problem. We are separated from God by our sin (Isaiah 59:1–2); in sin we fail to love Him.

The prophet Isaiah described God's suffering servant who was appointed to provide atonement for our sins by giving His own life (see Isaiah 52:13–53:12, especially 53:9–12). Paul, a former Pharisee who became a follower of Jesus (Acts 9:1–22), writes this about what the sacrificial death of Jesus did for those who trust in Him: "He made Him who knew no sin to be sin in our behalf, so that we might become the righteousness of God in Him" (2 Corinthians 5:21; see also 1 John 2:1–2).

The greatest and most needed of gifts, forgiveness of sin and eternal life, the Jewish Messiah freely gives to those who believe in Him. If you haven't already trusted in Jesus, won't you today let the God of Abraham, Isaac, and Jacob first repair you from the inside out? Then, you can love others as yourself with the very love of God as He makes you a "new creation" (2 Corinthians 5:17–20).

With so much heartache in our world, let us get the help and comfort we need from God so we can properly help others who need the same.

Application

What would it look like to put the love of Messiah first and then have Him empower you to fulfill the Golden Rule? Is there a "neighbor" in need of your love today?

Day 10

Beyond Bystanders

For God is not unjust so as to forget your work and the love which you have shown toward His name, by having served and by still serving the saints.
Hebrews 6:10

My jacket once saved my life.

As a child growing up in the Soviet Union, I was coming down the stairs of my elementary school one day when I heard the boys, my classmates, yelling racial slurs. They were coming for me.

Even at 11 years old, I knew antisemitism was something I had to endure. My classmates needed someone to blame for their trouble. I am Jewish, so I was the target.

The beating left me in a bleeding, bruised heap on the ground. I was injured but alive; the black jacket that sheltered me from the winter elements had provided just enough cushion to protect my internal organs.

They could have killed me.

Six months later, the beating endangered my life once more when it caused me to need emergency stomach surgery. Providentially, a visiting surgeon just happened to be at the remote hospital where I was taken. He was a godsend.

As my dear friend Lydia told me of her life in the former Soviet Union, my heart ached for her lost childhood. No child should have to endure such hatred. No wonder at age 18 Lydia convinced her family to leave. From 1987 to 1990, over 220,000 Jewish people, including Lydia's family, fled the Soviet Union.

The emigration process for the Jewish community was humiliating. Labeled as traitors, they were stripped of all identifying documents. Passports (identifying them not as "citizens" but as "Jews") were confiscated. Temporary visas labeled "refugee" were issued.

Juxtaposing my life with Lydia's reveals stark contrasts.

While Lydia was fleeing with her family to Italy, I was learning to swim.

While Lydia was learning a new language to ensure her survival, I was watching Saturday morning cartoons.

It is hard to relate to people whose life stories are drastically different from ours. To build bridges of understanding, we need to hear their stories. We need to enter their world. We need to demonstrate the love of Messiah Jesus.

The Jewish people have endured suffering for generations, often at the hands of professing Christians. It takes a courageous person to oppose baseless hatred – confronting one ugly comment or violent attack at a time.

But we can make our voices heard over the shouting. The consequences might mean we suffer alongside God's people. This is the model of Israel's Messiah Jesus, a man of suffering and acquainted with grief (Isaiah 53:3).

It would have only taken one person to stop Lydia's beating. Next time, let it not be a jacket that protects from the blows.

Application

Are you aware of the antisemitism (hatred of Jewish people) that exists in our world? Would you pray and ask God to show you how you can stand against antisemitism?

Day 11

Casting Away

He will again take pity on us; He will trample on our wrongdoings. Yes, You will cast all their sins Into the depths of the sea.
Micah 7:19

"Fall is about to show us how beautiful it is to let things go."
– Anonymous

Parenting taught me an essential art: the quick removal of potential choking hazards. Prying dangerous objects from grasping little fingers can be challenging; toddler tantrums often result.

With my little son it was a bit easier. When he found something too small for safe play, instead of beginning a wrestling match, I asked him to throw it to me. What little boy doesn't like to throw things? This practice resolved the immediate danger.

Teaching kids how to let go of something is a lesson that will hopefully follow them into adulthood. Often I still need to be reminded to let go of something harmful. Unforgiveness. Old habits. Resentment. Sin.

One late September day, as I stood near the shore enjoying a New York sunset, I witnessed a unique sight: hundreds of Orthodox Jewish children and adults were hurling pieces of bread into the rising Atlantic tide.

They were performing a customary atonement ritual called *tashlikh* (Hebrew for "cast off"). This annual ritual is done between Rosh Hashanah (the Jewish New Year) and Yom Kippur (the Day of Atonement). It is based on a Bible passage: "He will again have compassion on us; He will tread our iniquities under foot. You will cast all their sins into the depths of the sea" (Micah 7:19).

The Jewish families were symbolically throwing their sins into the water, never to be seen again. A picture of God's complete forgiveness.

But according to Scripture, forgiveness is grounded in an atoning sacrifice (Leviticus 16 and 17:11, and Hebrews 9:22 emphasize the necessity of blood for atonement). Yeshua, the perfect, spotless lamb of God, paid the penalty for our sins. He "tread our iniquities" under His foot when it was nailed to Calvary's tree. He made possible the Father's complete forgiveness of our transgressions. Our Messiah's once-for-all atonement was perfect (see Hebrews 10).

With this faith and knowledge, why do I still hold on to things I should let go, like the sins of others and hurtful things once spoken to me?

Sitting in my car some years ago, I cried out to God in prayer. A recent fallout with a friend had bankrupted me. Anger, hurt, and the ache of rejection flooded my mind. *How can I move past this hurt? I am stuck.* With hands clasped, I prayed to God for justice.

Quietly, an image of Messiah Jesus on the cross came to mind.

The powerful thought gripped me: *I have been given perfect justice.* I already enjoyed the reality that all *my* sins were forgiven. But would I accept that His sacrifice was also for the sins of others?

By holding onto unforgiveness and resentment, I was in turn rejecting Yeshua's sacrifice for the sins of others.

My heart ached within me at the thought. With hands wide open I released the offense and accepted perfect justice. *Tashlikh*. Casting away. *Thank you, Yeshua*.

Application

What are you holding on to that needs to be released to the nail-scarred hands of the Messiah?

Day 12

Kill the Carrot

*If we have food and covering,
with these we shall be content.
1 Timothy 6:8*

It's 11 at night and I'm scrolling through the endless void of Instagram. I know I should be sleeping. I'm annoyed that I'm dissatisfied and uninterested, and yet I continue.

Endless scrolling on social media reminds me of the verse "The eye is not satisfied with seeing, nor is the ear filled with hearing" (Ecclesiastes 1:8). There is always just…one…more…thing…to…see. A carrot dangling in front of my face.

Our society is baited by consumerism, and technology feeds our insatiable desires. I have begun to realize it has trained the way I think; discontentment trickles over into other areas of my life.

The image of the carrot and the stick comes from 19th-century literature. The earliest carrot-and-stick narrative came from a traveler's story of his journey through Russia in 1890: "As I rode along, there flashed into my mind a cartoon I had once seen of a donkey race in which the victory had been won by an ingenious jockey who held a carrot on the end of a stick a foot or two in front of his donkey's nose." Instead of beating the donkey with the stick, the jockey had placed something delicious just outside of his mount's reach.

Attraction is often a better motivator than force, though sometimes both techniques work together. Winston Churchill described Hitler's tactics in 1938 this way: "Thus, by every device from the stick to the carrot, the emaciated Austrian donkey is made to pull the Nazi barrow up an ever-steepening hill."

Persuasion and manipulation are the Adversary's mother tongue. He has taught the world's systems to apply his strategies for thousands of years. He deceived Adam and Eve into thinking there was something better than what God provided. The carrot swung in front of them and they grasped for it, envisioning a better life... only to find they had lost everything.

Being content is an age-old Jewish concern. The phrase *samayach b'chelko* means "contentment with one's lot or portion."

The Jewish community translates Proverbs 15:15 thus: "All the days of a poor person are wretched, but contentment is a feast without end."

I'm pretty sure this verse is not referring to the monetary status of poor versus rich; one can have all the money in the world and still be poor and wretched. The limitless images we see every day paint a picture of a better life...if only. If only I had a nicer home, a happier family, a more fulfilling job, more fashionable clothes.

A continual feast of if-only carrots leads to poverty. Happiness with *more* is a mirage.

Kill the carrot.

The wealthiest people I've met have been those who exercised contentment and were at peace with what they had been given. Joy comes when we stop, look up, and see all we have been given. A thanksgiving feast awaits those who exercise contentment.

And the Creator smiles.

Application

What are a few of your personal "carrots"? What do they indicate about your relationship with Jesus?

Day 13

To Be Satisfied

*As a result of the anguish of His soul, He will
see it and be satisfied;
By His knowledge the Righteous One, My
Servant, will justify the many,
For He will bear their wrongdoings.
Isaiah 53:11*

Ice cream on a hot summer's day. Warming yourself by the fire during the first snow. Taking your socks and shoes off after a long day on your feet.

What do all these things have in common? For me, they all bring some level of satisfaction. *To satisfy* means to meet the needs, desires, or expectations of someone. When I think of being satisfied, I think of receiving something good. I find satisfaction when my eight-month-old puppy obeys my command. I am satisfied when I get a good job-performance review. I was satisfied with the chocolate brownie I ordered at a restaurant last night.

But is this all there is to satisfaction?

Recently, I was teaching the youth of my church that Jesus is fully God, yet fully man. He has both a divine nature and a human nature. Only His sacrifice provides full atonement for our sins.

Many of my students were learning this for the first time and I could see that it resonated with them. Yet their main takeaway was not the Messiah's two natures. Rather, it was that Jesus wanted to give His life for their sake, that He desired to suffer for them. Sure, these kids had heard that only Jesus' atonement was sufficient to cover their sins. But the fact that He wanted to give His everything for them? That was incredible.

I often speak about what was accomplished on the cross nearly two millennia ago – this event is so incredibly important! Yet I too easily forget that this act, Jesus' death, was pleasing to God. Many of us fear death. We avoid the topic. Yet Jesus' death delighted God.

In Isaiah 53 we read how God's suffering servant was despised and rejected, how He was beaten and crushed and killed with the wicked, yet buried in a rich man's tomb. Isaiah says that it was the will of the Lord to crush the servant.

And after being despised, rejected, beaten, crushed, and ultimately killed, "As a result of the anguish of His soul, [the Messiah] will see it and be satisfied" (Isaiah 53:11).

May the truth of Messiah's sacrifice be proclaimed for all to hear! And as we walk with Him, suffer with Him, and minister with Him, may His delight over His own suffering be an encouragement to us.

Because satisfaction is much deeper than a warm brownie, an ice cream cone, or even an obedient puppy. True, whole, and lasting satisfaction is found only in the One who gave His life for us – and was satisfied to do so.

Application

Have you ever read the prophecy of the suffering servant in Isaiah 53? Read it and meditate on the fact that Jesus was willing to suffer for our sake, and was satisfied with the result.

Day 14

The God Who Sees

Then she called the name of the Lord who spoke to her, "You are a God who sees me"; for she said, "Have I even seen Him here and lived after He saw me?"
Genesis 16:13

Esther's patent leather shoes clicked on the wet sidewalk as she window-shopped, her reflection bouncing off the glass. As she hurried home, the normal street traffic of her ultra-Orthodox Jewish community buzzed around her.

Esther was lost in thought when a gust of wind pushed against her cheek, disrupting her tidy wig. She caught it and tucked the strand behind her ear. The love and hard work she poured out for her family was evident in the load of groceries and packages she carried.

Esther headed up the first flight of stairs to her family's apartment. Thoughts of dinner preparation consumed her mind. At the door, she instinctively reached toward the *mezuzah* and then drew her fingers to her lips.

Inside, Esther poured herself some tea, savoring the quiet before the children came home from school. Then she noticed the *frum* (Yiddish for "pious") community newspaper lying open on the table. It highlighted a plea on behalf of a young family who had lost their mother to cancer. *Tzedakah* (charity) could be given for the surviving husband and six children.

The heartbreaking story pulled at Esther's emotions, but what really stung her was the family photo: The children were pictured standing like stairsteps, each about a year apart in age. Their deceased mother had been photoshopped out of the background; an empty white space remained where she had sat.

Esther slumped into her chair and covered her face.

Due to *tznius* (modesty laws), the ultra-Orthodox community does not picture women in their publications. It is seen as a way of protecting women from being objectified. Unfortunately, this law, meant to protect women, is the very tool that objectifies them.

The mother's erased face left Esther wondering, *Who was this unseen woman? Did she have laugh lines? What bright eyes and gentle manner do her children now ache for? With her image removed, she already seems forgotten.*

We read in Scripture of Hagar (Genesis 16), who, at the suggestion of her barren mistress Sarai, becomes

Abram's concubine and gets pregnant with his child. When Sarai turns against her and drives her away, Hagar's circumstances are decided for her. Humiliated, exiled, and exhausted, she is beside a spring of water in the wilderness when God finds her.

For the first time in Scripture, we see "Angel of the LORD" (YHWH) used (Genesis 16:7). The Angel of the Lord is a special messenger from God who speaks for and is closely identified with Him. According to the Amplified Study Bible notes, "Many scholars believe this Angel may be a theophany, that is, a physical manifestation of God. The Angel of the LORD, based on context, may be the pre-incarnate Messiah, the Son of God."

It astonishes me that the first time this messenger is mentioned in Scripture, He is sent to an unseen, enslaved woman. He speaks kindly to her troubled soul and prophesies over her unborn child, telling her to return home. Hagar then names this messenger *El Roi* – "He sees, He is aware, He is the great Omnipresent God" (AMP). She believes she has just seen the Lord.

Verse 13 reads: "Then she called the name of the LORD who spoke to her, 'You are God Who Sees'; for she said, 'Have I not even here [in the wilderness] remained alive after seeing Him [who sees me with understanding and compassion]?'" (Amplified Bible).

The God who sees me.

He is the Living God who looks on us with understanding and compassion. This unseen God makes Himself known to us through His Messenger. Jesus the Messiah's recorded history in the gospels reveals to us that He saw people. Jesus went through Samaria to meet the woman at the well (John 4). He had mercy on a blind man in Jericho, restoring his sight (Luke 18:35–43).

Trouble comes when we believe we are forgotten and that God is aloof. We fall into despair and sin. Hope is restored when we encounter Him and we see Him.

Looking for signs of God at work has become a source of joy for me. Sometimes I see Him working quietly on the outskirts of my life. My heart leaps when I make the connection between His work and my circumstances.

When we behold Him, we in turn become more like Him, and we end up *seeing* others.

To the Orthodox woman hidden in your society...I see you. To the tired student, trying your best this semester...I see you. To the exhausted husband working to make ends meet...I see you. To the one loaded with the crushing weight of your circumstances...I see you.

I see you because He sees you. He has not forgotten you.

Application

Would you pray for the many people who feel unseen by God and by others? Especially pray for women in the ultra-Orthodox community, that God would bring light into their lives through Messiah Jesus.

Day 15

Tasting God

*Taste and see that
the LORD is good;
How blessed is the man
who takes refuge in Him!
Psalm 34:8*

The beauty, majesty, and vastness of the mountains in Aspen, Colorado, were like a fragrant hyacinth to my New York City-born soul. Skiing in this heaven on earth was a dream come true; just one ski season here made an Aspen evangelist of me.

Where does this evangelistic zeal come from? People naturally promote the objects of their passion, whether a sport, sports team, grandchild, book, recipe, restaurant, blog, movie, or political candidate. No one told me, "Go home to your people and make disciples of Aspen and snow skiing." I simply wanted everyone to experience what I had tasted, and I wasted no opportunity to point others to those snow-covered slopes.

Israel's most famous king was just such an evangelist. King David was passionate, but not for something as dull as the Rockies or banal as skiing. He wanted everyone to experience what he had experienced – God's prayer-answering, fear-relieving, shame-lifting, trouble-saving, camp-encircling, soul-cleansing Self. David's personal experience of God compelled him to sing this invitation: "Taste and see that the LORD is good; how blessed is the man who takes refuge in Him!" (Psalm 34:8).

David "tasted" the infinite God by walking through life with Him. David's psalms describe his experience of tasting God's goodness. His use of words like "magnify," "exalt," "look to," "cry," "take refuge," and "fear" – a reverential awe for God's power – picture David's daily dependence on God's involvement in every happy and hard event in his life. His choice of words like "praise," "rejoice," "exult," "hallelujah," and "overflow" picture the happy benefits of tasting God's goodness.

David's invitation sums up our passion at Life in Messiah: a longing for God's Jewish people to taste the riches of God's goodness in Messiah, and for His Church to taste the wonders of God's plan for Israel and all His sin-battered creation.

When you read David's psalms, do you relate to his overwhelming awe and gratitude for God's goodness? Have you, too, tasted the "width and length and height and depth" of God's love (Ephesians 3:18–19)? Don't you long for others to experience the blessings of knowing God?

Taste His goodness more fully by enriching your appreciation of His abiding passion for redeeming His Jewish people – and your critical role, as a believer in Jesus, in spreading the Good News.

You have little to lose and everything to gain when you encourage unbelievers to "taste and see that the LORD is good."

How happy you will be!

Application

Which one of your friends needs to taste and see God's goodness? How would the Lord have you reach out to them?

Day 16

The Remark

*Listen to advice and accept discipline,
So that you may be wise the rest of your days.
Proverbs 19:20*

"Look, I'm not trying to be offensive, but after all, he is a Jew."

It was a beautiful winter afternoon in southern Israel, the thermometer climbing toward 80 degrees. I was sitting in a youth hostel with a group of about 10 people. We were an international smorgasbord of cultures, all meeting for the first time.

Among us were a young Israeli woman who had recently finished her military service, a youthful German college student on vacation, a 20-something, shy French Jewish man traveling to Israel for his first time; a boisterous, extroverted man, William, from the UK; and a handful of others from various countries, including myself.

Spontaneous gatherings like this are the charm that draws some travelers to lodge in hostels. Social interaction in a hostel is unavoidable, and as people strike up conversations, often others join. Soon one finds oneself engaged in conversations with topics and perspectives that may be enriching and challenging.

Each grabbing a cup of coffee or tea, our group was soon comfortably chatting with each other. Our interaction, punctuated with frequent laughter, included tips on where to go while in Israel, questions about one another's backgrounds, and comparison of cultures.

At one point, as the young Israeli woman finished sharing a story, the details of which I do not recall, William made the remark I do recall: "I'm not trying to be offensive, but after all, he is a Jew."

No one had seen this coming – a sudden bucket of ice dumped on a warm chat. I scanned everyone's eyes as silence gripped us. My first glance was at the young Israeli woman, who looked almost apologetic for possibly inviting the remark. The German student stared at the ground. The shy Frenchman appeared nonplussed, his awkward look saying, "Let's act like nothing happened." Others shifted nervously. The man who had made the remark seemed oblivious, as though we were all mates in a pub who would laugh or nod in agreement.

Inside, my mind screamed, *That was not okay*. My thoughts raced. Should I react strongly? Confront him? Be the voice of outrage, accusing and shaming him? I remained silent, assessing. The man who had made the remark truly had no clue he had offended anyone. He stood up and said, "I'm for another tea. Can I get something for anyone else?"

This was my chance. I followed him to the large hot water urn where the cups, tea, and instant coffee sat on a table. Smiling, he offered to make tea or coffee for me.

This is the moment. "Hi, William," I said. "We haven't really met formally. Is it okay if we sit and talk a few minutes?"

He readily assented. As we sat down, I noticed some of the others were still chatting where we had left them. The young Israeli woman was looking at her phone. She glanced toward us for a moment, perhaps curious.

As I confronted William with his offensive remark, he offered no defense, no pushback, no excuses. He seemed as stunned by my words as we had been by his. My initial outrage at William for his insensitivity turned to pity.

We had a long, fruitful conversation. Then I silently thanked God as William, with no prompting from me, stood up and walked straight over to the young Israeli woman. I could not hear their conversation, but even from a distance I could see their emotion expressed in a conciliatory hug.

I talked with William a few more times over the next couple of days. On one occasion I smiled when I heard him speaking with a small group who had arrived at the hostel, informing them of his past ignorance in how he had spoken about Jewish people. He now wanted to help others avoid the negative Jewish stereotypes he had accepted for years.

In the past two decades, the Jewish community in areas around the world has experienced an alarming rise in antisemitism, especially in North America and Europe, where the largest diaspora communities dwell. On social networks, hateful speech and anti-Jewish tropes soaked in a history of antisemitism are far too common. Far worse are the physical assaults suffered by individuals simply because they are Jewish. And it's not getting better.

These are times when believers need to be strong voices against this oldest hatred, wherever it is encountered – whether in publications, on social media, or in person. Racism in any form is an offense against our Lord's command to love one another. How utterly wrong to claim to love Jesus and yet to hate His people!

These are times when we need to lovingly confront others for the insensitive or antisemitic ways they speak about the Jewish people. What a victory when someone like William not only ceases their offensive ways of speaking, but also understands the pain and damage they have caused and seeks to rectify it. A biblical proverb comes to mind: "Listen to counsel, receive instruction, and accept correction, that you may be wise in the time to come" (Proverbs 19:20).

Application

What instances of racism, including antisemitism, have you witnessed? How will you respond when the Holy Spirit prompts you to stand up for those being insulted, abused, or worse?

Day 17

A Great Gift from Small Faith

*The Law of the LORD is perfect,
restoring the soul;
The testimony of the LORD is sure,
making wise the simple.
Psalms 19:7*

The day was beautiful, not a cloud in the crisp, clear blue sky. I sat enjoying the warmth as I read. It was easy to ignore the background noise of the city.

Then a voice pulled me from my thoughts. "Hello, sorry to interrupt; is that a Bible you're reading?"

I looked up. The question came from a young man, likely in his mid-to-late 20s, who was sitting quietly on a nearby bench. He smiled when I told him, "Yes, it is. Do you read the Bible?"

"Not very often – but I know I should," he responded.

Soon we were in a warm discussion; he was eager to talk. I found out he was the son of an Orthodox rabbi but that he himself was currently "off the path" (not observing his religion). He explained that he only practiced his faith around his family. Now living on his own, he found it difficult to live religiously because, "I do not know if I really even believe in God."

Time seemed to fly by and stand still at the same time. Whether it lasted one hour or two, I only know that our discussion seemed divinely appointed.

My new acquaintance asked me, "What religion are you? A Christian?"

I replied that I preferred to call my myself a "follower of Jesus" or "believer in Jesus." This caught his attention. He asked, "Why?"

What followed was not only a discussion on the sad and bloody history of the persecution of Jewish people by Christians throughout European history; we also discussed my love for Israel and the Jewish people and my desire for all people to come to know the God of Abraham, Isaac, and Jacob!

I grew excited as I talked about the truth and God's plan as revealed in the Old Testament. Starting with creation and the disobedience of Adam and Eve, we discussed the pictures of the future painted through the patriarchs and prophets of Israel (Genesis 3:1–24, 4:1–7, 22:1–18, 49:10, 50:15–21), and the promises especially of a prophet like Moses (Deuteronomy 18:15), a special servant (Isaiah 42:1–9, 49:1–8) and the One called God's Son (Psalm 2:1–12, Proverbs 30:1–5, Genesis 22:2, John 3:16, Isaiah 9:6–7).

After quite some time, the young man said, "I have never looked at the *Tanakh* (Old Testament) or Torah like you are talking about. For me, it was just part of my religion. But you really believe it, know it, and study it with joy, it seems. The things you are showing in my Bible I never saw or knew were there."

He added, "What you say really makes sense and I can understand how you can believe Jesus is the Messiah. I wish I could have the kind of faith you have."

I told him I did not have great faith, but I had simply received a great gift with a small amount of faith (Luke 17:6, Ephesians 2:8–9). God could and would do the same for him if he was willing to receive the gift.

The following day I went to the same spot and once again, the young man was sitting where he had been the previous day. We greeted one another warmly.

He immediately began telling me he had read some of the passages in the *Tanakh* I had spoken of (Isaiah 52:13–53:12, Ezekiel 36:24–26, Jeremiah 31:33–34, Psalm 110:1–4, 22:1–31; John 3:1–18). He had difficulty believing that the rabbis, like his father, did not see what he saw. *There has to be more to it*, he thought. Turns out he had studied the Oral Law (rabbinic tradition and commentaries on the Old Testament) but never the Bible.

Before the young man left, I issued a challenge. "I am certain God gave us the Scriptures to read, study, and understand on our own, and not just assume they mean what religious leaders say they mean," I said. "God communicates the truth to us individually as we learn how to study...so please, keep on reading. My challenge is for you to ask God to show you He is real; and if Jesus is the promised Messiah, that He will reveal to you that you can also receive the gift He wants to give you: your wish of greater faith!"

Application

Do you have questions regarding Jesus and how the Old Testament clearly points to Him? Will you study the passages mentioned in this article and ask God your questions today?

Day 18

"My Rabbi Told Me Not To"

...But you will receive power when the Holy Spirit has come upon you; and you shall be My witnesses both in Jerusalem and in all Judea, and Samaria, and as far as the remotest part of the earth.
Acts 1:8

My sandals were wet as we exited Hezekiah's Tunnel (2 Chronicles 32:30 and 2 Kings 20:20 tells how Judah's king constructed the tunnel in the eighth century BC to protect Jerusalem's water supply from the Assyrian army). After we ascended to the southwest corner of the Temple Mount, my wife engaged an Israeli named Issachar in conversation. I joined as she offered him a copy of *Betrayed!* by Stan Telchin. We told him it was the testimony of a Jewish father who came to faith in Jesus after reading the New Testament.

Issachar politely declined, saying, "My rabbi told me not to read Christian material."

When I heard his reason for declining the book, I was not surprised; my heart sinks every time I hear it. Sensing the Spirit's nudge, I kindly challenged Issachar: "Do you really want your rabbi telling you what to read and not read?"

"I trust him," Issachar responded. "He is very smart and studies all the time."

"What if he is wrong? The rabbis disagree with each other all the time, don't they?"

"Yes, sometimes," he admitted, then added, "I have been really curious about the New Testament. But it's forbidden to read it. I want to, but I am not allowed."

"But it's a Jewish book, written by your people," I said.

"My rabbi told me not to," Issachar insisted.

I persisted. "I am normally not this direct with people, but I think you are giving too much control to your rabbi. Are you willing to place that much trust in him? Has he ever read the New Testament?"

"I will ask him about this, but I don't think he will like it," said Issachar.

We ended our exchange with a smile and friendly handshake.

Issachar is not alone in his reason for not reading the New Testament or other Christian material. Thousands of our religious Jewish friends are taught to never investigate the New Testament for themselves. Their rabbis tell them God will strike them dead if they even enter a church.

Sadly, the broader secular segment of the Jewish population also is often influenced by the Jewish religious authorities. Many Jewish people are taught that Jesus came to start a new religion. Others believe the New Testament is antisemitic. These misrepresentations hinder Jewish people from learning the truth about the Jewish King of Israel, the Messiah.

What can we do to advance the truth about Jesus among our Jewish friends? I'll offer two truths to remember as you consider ways you can make an impact this very day.

First, remember that Israel has a zeal for God, but not according to knowledge (Romans 10:1–4). The knowledge they lack is the Good News that righteousness is by faith in Messiah, not the works of man.

Many Jewish people think they know about Jesus, but most do not. Some have no idea that Jesus is even Jewish! Few have heard a clear gospel presentation. Most have little to no idea what the New Testament teaches, or that it was largely written by Jewish writers.

In light of these realities, please share the Good News with your Jewish friends and offer them a New Testament. If you are not going to do it, who will?

Second, Paul earnestly prayed for the salvation of Israel (Romans 10:1–4). We should do the same. Pray for Jewish individuals like Issachar, who desire to investigate the claims of Jesus but are afraid to do so.

Robert Murray M'Cheyne once traveled abroad to bring the Good News to the Jewish people. On November 17, 1839, he preached the sermon "Our Duty to Israel," in which he stated:

> All that we plead for is, that, in sending out missionaries to the heathen, we may not forget to begin at Jerusalem. If Paul be sent to the gentile, let Peter be sent to the twelve tribes that are scattered abroad; and let not a bye-corner in your hearts be given to this cause – let it not be an appendix to the other doings of our Church, but rather let there be written on the fore front of your hearts, and on the banner of our beloved Church, "To the Jew first," and "Beginning at Jerusalem."

May the beloved church never forget her beginnings. And may we never cease to bring Messiah's message to His Jewish people.

Application

Would you pray and ask God to show you ways you can take the truth of the gospel to the Jewish people living around you?

Day 19

Fear of the Known

There is no fear in love, but perfect love drives out fear, because fear involves punishment, and the one who fears is not perfected in love.
1 John 4:18

A small group of college students had gathered for the weekly Bible study I taught on campus. I had just finished praying for our study time when the door slowly opened...but no one entered.

I called out, "Please, come in and join us."

After a slight pause, a young woman in her early 20s slowly entered the room. Her dark, shoulder-length hair wreathed her curious expression.

Within minutes I found out that Leah had seen a publicly posted invitation for our Messianic Bible study and had wanted to see what it was about. She was Jewish, and her father was a Reform rabbi.

"You came on the perfect day, Leah," I told her. "We are going to look at Messianic prophecies from the *Tanakh* (Old Testament)."

Leah seemed unsure of herself. Thankfully, the group that day was small, and a Christian student about her age made her feel quite welcome. For the next 45 minutes we turned to passages from various books of the Old Testament. Leah seemed to hang on every word. Her eyes were glued to the Bible she'd been given.

Finally, we arrived at Isaiah 53. I mentioned that, over the centuries, opinions had differed on whom this chapter was speaking about: a person? the Messiah of Israel? the people of Israel? or Isaiah himself?

"But I believe that by the end of the chapter it will be obvious who this chapter is speaking of," I stated. Verse by verse, I carefully explained the text, pointing to historical truths and other Scripture passages that indicated the identity of the person in Isaiah 53.

As we progressed, Leah stared at the Bible with focused intensity, her fingers following the text. Her lips moved as if she was silently talking to herself.

I spoke of the picture Isaiah was painting of this rejected servant who was falsely accused, scorned, and even killed. And God Himself was pleased because of what this servant's suffering and death accomplished.

Leah asked a simple question: "Why don't the rabbis teach this?"

I responded, "I could give you my opinion, but why don't you ask your father?"

We examined the details at the end of the chapter. This remarkable servant saw life again after death, making forgiveness of sin possible.

Glancing at Leah, I saw an unmistakable look: fear was evident in her countenance as she suddenly realized who Isaiah 53 was about. I silently prayed for her. Then, as I opened my mouth to speak, Leah stiffened. She quickly closed the Bible. Without a word, she stood up and practically fled out the door.

After that memorable evening, I saw Leah a few more times on campus, but she never acknowledged me. I always wondered what she did with the fear she experienced that day.

The Bible teaches us that "perfect love drives out fear" (1 John 4:14–18). If you have placed your faith in His Son as your Savior, then you can say with confidence, "The Lord is my helper; I will not be afraid. What will man do to me?" (Hebrews 13:6).

Application

Pray for Jewish people like Leah, who have realized that Jesus is the fulfillment of the Old Testament prophecies but are afraid to take the step of believing in Him.

Day 20

The Language of Truth

*Open my eyes, that I may behold
Wonderful things from Your Law.
I am a stranger on the earth;
Do not hide Your commandments from me.
Psalm 119:18–19*

"Do you understand Hebrew?"

The pointed question came from an Orthodox Jewish man who was passing by on a busy city street. He had taken offense at my handing tracts to the people going by, many of whom were Jewish.

Looking at the tract, he had noticed that Isaiah 52:13–53:12 was quoted in both Hebrew and English. His immediate response was to challenge my ability to understand the meaning of the text in its original language. If I wasn't fluent in Hebrew, what right did I have to hand this tract to passersby?

I readily admitted my knowledge of biblical Hebrew was minimal. I asked if that meant I could not understand the meaning of Isaiah's words in the English translation.

This was the only question I was able to ask. Instead of replying to it, the man engaged in a passionate, and seemingly prepared, list of reasons of why he pitied me in my ignorance. Not only was I deceived, he said, but I was perpetuating this deception among Jewish people.

I'm not naive about why he was opposed to what I was doing. Isaiah 53 is the clearest description of Messiah in the Hebrew Scriptures (Old Testament). Even though I had not mentioned Jesus yet, my Orthodox friend did so numerous times in his impassioned monologue. His lecture completed, he turned on his heel and departed.

After he walked away, I thought deeply about his words. I had wanted to tell him that I agreed that a fluent understanding of biblical Hebrew would surely bless me with even richer, deeper insight and appreciation for the Scriptures – which we both agreed are God's Word.

I had wanted to ask if he believed that only people who knew Hebrew could understand the meaning of the *Tanakh* (Old Testament), or if he believed there had never been language experts or scholars capable of accurately translating the Hebrew text into other languages.

I could sympathize with this man's opposition to the belief that Jesus is the promised Jewish Messiah; I understood that his rejection of Jesus was reinforced by some of history's worst examples of hatred toward, and murder of, Jewish people at the hands of people who claimed Christianity. I also thought how difficult it must be to believe in Jesus when, for centuries, the great majority of the most learned Jewish leaders have rejected Jesus as the Messiah.

There are numerous examples of Jewish people through the centuries who have believed that Jesus is the promised Messiah of Israel. Today we see a growing number of Messianic Jews who have trusted in Jesus and are maintaining a strong Jewish identity, despite continued rejection from their kinsmen. Some Jewish believers are well-versed in Hebrew, but many are not.

The question remains: is facility with the original languages (Hebrew and Aramaic for the Old Testament, Koine Greek for the New Testament) necessary to understand the truth of God's Word?

Not in a day when we have access to accurate translations of Scripture in so many of the world's languages. Biblical scholars have invested their lives in translating God's Word into the heart languages of people around the world.

God's truth was meant for all people to understand and embrace, regardless of their language. In Psalm 119:160, the Psalmist writes, "The sum of Your word is truth, and every one of Your righteous judgments is everlasting."

After identifying Jesus as the Word, the disciple John wrote these very telling words regarding truth: "And the Word became flesh, and dwelt among us; and we saw His glory, glory as of the only Son from the Father, full of grace and truth" (John 1:14). He then added these words: "For the Law was given through Moses; grace and truth were realized through Jesus Christ" (John 1:17).

Understanding truth is not limited to knowing a particular language, especially when it comes to God's Word. His redemptive plan is clearly laid out in the Scriptures, fulfilled by the One who fully embodies Truth. Jesus claimed, "I am the way, and the truth, and the life; no one comes to the Father except through Me" (John 14:6).

The study of other languages is a wonderful pursuit that enriches our understanding of the world. But rest assured, you can come to the knowledge of God's truth in a language other than Hebrew, Aramaic, or Greek. The greater challenge is to approach the text of Scripture – in whatever language we speak – in a spirit of humility, asking the Divine Author to help us both comprehend and believe what He has preserved for us.

Application

What obstacles does the Evil One put in the way of you sharing your faith? Perhaps you're afraid someone will ask a question you can't answer. Take courage! You don't need to be a Hebrew scholar to share your personal story of faith.

Day 21

Provoked to Jealousy

Therefore insofar as I am an apostle of Gentiles, I magnify my ministry if somehow I may move my own people to jealousy and save some of them.
Romans 11:13–14

It was a hot day in Israel. We were in Eilat, a southern city on the Red Sea, where the summer temperature regularly exceeds 100 degrees Fahrenheit. On this particular day, we found ourselves on the Eilat Promenade, a long boardwalk filled with shops, restaurants, carnival rides, and people. As we walked the Promenade, our group sang songs, distributed tracts, and conversed with people about the gospel.

After a few hours, we sought refuge from the heat inside one of the air-conditioned restaurants strung along the promenade.

Shortly after we sat down, a young Israeli girl named Orna asked if she could sit in one of the open chairs at our table.

"Absolutely," we told her.

She sat down and explained, "You guys have the only seat left with a place to charge my cell phone." She made herself comfortable. After some small talk, Orna asked us why we were in Israel.

"We flew all the way from the US to Israel because we love the God of Israel," we explained. "We want the people of Israel to know about their Messiah, Yeshua."

Orna was surprised. She explained that a friend from Canada had been sharing things about Jesus with her. After a while, one of our team members quoted some Scripture to Orna about God and the Jewish people.

I will never forget what happened next. Orna's eyes welled up with tears. She looked at us seriously and said, "I am embarrassed that you guys, who are Gentiles, know my Scriptures better than I do."

What was going on inside Orna? Paul describes it like this: "...salvation has come to the Gentiles, to make [Israel] jealous" (Romans 11:11).

Orna saw that a group of Gentiles loved the people of Israel. She was surprised at how well we knew the Bible (which was written by her ancestors under the inspiration of the Holy Spirit). She saw the fruit of the Spirit within us (Galatians 5:9). Orna wanted what we had. She was provoked to jealousy!

In Romans 11, Paul explains God's wonderful plans for both the Gentiles and the Jewish people. One important point (among many) is that God has granted salvation to the Gentiles in order to provoke Israel into seeking a restored relationship with Himself.

Several times Paul warns Gentiles not to be arrogant, conceited, or unaware of God's plans for Israel (Romans 11:18–25). I can't help but think about the many times in history that the Jewish people have been provoked by Christians. Unfortunately, many of these provocations have not been the kind of loving provocations Paul described.

Rather, Christian provocation has often been hateful and hurtful to the Jewish community, coming from the arrogance and ignorance that Paul warned against.

God is actively moving among the Jewish people today. Young Israelis are searching for spiritual truth. More and more, evangelicals are learning about God's heart for the Jewish people. Many Christians are reading Romans 9–11 and coming to understand God's plan for Israel and the nations. This is an incredible time to be in Jewish ministry!

Application

We don't know how long the door to sharing the gospel with Israelis will remain open. Will you join us as we seek to "provoke" the Jewish people into a relationship with their Jewish Messiah?

Day 22

Planting Seeds, Tilling Soil

*I will open rivers on the bare heights,
And springs in the midst of the valleys;
I will make the wilderness a pool of water,
And the dry land fountains of water.
Isaiah 41:18*

There it was: a beautiful scene representing deep, spiritual truths. The long strip of verdant green shrubbery wound its way through the Negev desert until it gently touched the blue sky. It seemed unlikely that this narrow strip of shrubs and grass could survive the rocky, parched desert. It existed only because of the wadis, dry stream beds that collected the rain and funneled it to feed the desert greenery.

It was beautiful to see life amidst this rocky, parched land. As I continued my journey through the barren Israeli desert, I imagined the parched ground being replaced with forests, fields of flowers, rushing waterfalls, and wildlife drinking from calm, flowing streams.

The prophet Isaiah describes a time when God will "pour water on the thirsty land and streams on the dry ground…" (Isaiah 44:3). Ezekiel also describes a day when Israel will bloom, when the Dead Sea will support life and fruit trees will grow in the desert (Ezekiel 47:1–12). Imagine the Dead Sea teeming with life!

This is also a time when Israel will bloom spiritually. In Isaiah 44:3, God says, "I will pour out My Spirit on your offspring, and My blessing on your descendants." Paul alludes to this coming spiritual revival in Romans 11:26, when he writes, "…all Israel will be saved." Paul envisions a national revival for Israel, no doubt gleaned in part from his reading of Isaiah and Ezekiel.

However, you might point out, *these things are yet future*. Israel's desert is still a barren wasteland. The Dead Sea has no life. Israel's people have not been spiritually revived. Instead, they are a people who, by and large, do not know the Lord. What we can do *now*?

We can be busy preparing the soil for rain. We should be planting seeds by sharing the gospel and tilling the soil through prayer and loving-kindness in preparation for the coming spiritual rain (Zechariah 12:10).

Did you know Jewish ministry is the only ministry in which fruit is promised? The Bible tells us there will always be a "remnant according to God's gracious choice" (Romans 11:5), just as there was in Elijah's day (1 Kings 19:18). What does it look like to plant seeds and prepare soil with the hopeful expectation of bearing fruit – both present and future?

I believe there are three essential ways we can show love to Israel: through prayer (Romans 10:1), evangelism (Romans 1:16), and acts of kindness (Romans 11:11, 15:27).

Prophecies about the spiritual revival of Israel, spoken of by so many of the prophets and New Testament writers, should spur us to action! We do not presume to attempt speeding up God's sovereign timetable or hasten the return of the Messiah, but we know that someday all Israel will be saved, and we have an opportunity to contribute toward that end.

As I meet Israelis from different backgrounds, I am amazed at their openness to talk about Yeshua (Jesus) and the Bible. Of course, not everyone is open. Will you join Life in Messiah in prayer, evangelism, and other acts of love toward Israel and Jewish communities around the globe? With antisemitism on the rise across the globe, there is no better time to begin than now. The task will be easier if we all till and plant together. Ask God how He wants to use you to reach His people, the "apple of His eye" (Zechariah 2:8).

There is rain on the horizon.

Application

How can you pray for, share the gospel with, and show acts of kindness and love toward the Jewish people?

Ask God to show you which of these areas He wants you to focus on.

Day 23

Who's Really Converting?

...We worship what we do know, because salvation is from the Jews. But a time is coming, and even now has arrived, when the true worshipers will worship the Father in spirit and truth; for such people the Father seeks to be His worshipers.
John 4:22b–23

At a missions conference I attended one year, I struck up a conversation with another conference-goer between sessions. As Ken and I discussed the conference, I mentioned that I was on staff with Life in Messiah.

Ken reacted enthusiastically. "It must be exciting to convert Jews!" he said.

Ken's response was well-meant, but it still made me wince. He was expressing a prevalent belief that I've encountered for years: the idea that Jewish people who believe in Jesus are "converting." This may seem like an innocuous idea, but it's based on some problematic perspectives.

First, this idea is theologically flawed. The perspective that believers convert *anyone* misunderstands our role as Jesus' representatives. None of us are called to "convert" unbelievers; our responsibility is simply to spread the seeds of the gospel. God is the one who brings the seeds to harvest (1 Corinthians 3:6–7).

Second, this terminology is culturally insensitive. It evokes the horrible historical practice of forced conversion. Used by various religions at different times in history, this practice was especially popular in Christian Europe, where Jewish individuals were often compelled to profess Christianity and revoke their Jewishness under threat of death or expulsion. The word "convert" has a very different connotation for Jewish people whose ancestors were the victims of these practices.

Third, this idea is just fundamentally inaccurate. When we talk about converting, we typically mean changing from one religious system to another. Jewish people who come to faith in Jesus don't need to convert in this sense. They simply need to repent of their sin and return to the biblical roots of their faith in recognizing that Jesus is the Messiah who was promised in the Old Testament (see Genesis 3:15, Deuteronomy 18:15, Psalms 2, 22, 110; Isaiah 9:6–7, 11:1–12, 52:13–53:12; Micah 5:2, Zechariah 9:9, 12:10).

We see the Jewish roots of our faith in the Gospels, where belief in Jesus emerges within a Jewish context (see Matthew 1:1, 10:5–6, 15:24). Jesus, teaching Jewish people almost exclusively, is revealed as the long-awaited Jewish Messiah and the fulfillment of Jewish Law (Matthew 5:17–20).

It is only at the conclusion of His earthly ministry that Jesus explicitly charges His disciples to proclaim the Good News to the world. He commands a group of Jewish men, "Go, therefore, and make disciples of all the nations, baptizing them in the name of the Father and the Son and the Holy Spirit, teaching them to follow all that I commanded you" (Matthew 28:19–20a).

In Acts, we see the Jewish disciples traveling to the Gentile nations to proclaim the news of a God who cannot be seen and a Messiah whom the Gentiles have never heard of. The Gentile nations were unaware, until Jewish "missionaries" told them, that the Jewish Messiah had come and had died for them as well as for Israel. If Jesus isn't the Jewish Messiah, He isn't anyone's messiah!

In short, it is not Jewish believers who convert to an alien faith, but Gentile believers who, through Jesus, convert to faith in the God of Abraham, Isaac, and Jacob!

In Romans 11, Paul, the Jewish apostle to the Gentiles, addresses this issue and also gives a warning:

> But if some of the branches were broken off, and you, being a wild olive, were grafted in among them and became a partaker with them of the rich

root of the olive tree, do not be arrogant toward the branches; but if you are arrogant, remember that it is not you who supports the root, but the root supports you.... And they also, if they do not continue in their unbelief, will be grafted in; for God is able to graft them in again. For if you were cut off from what is by nature a wild olive tree, and contrary to nature were grafted into a cultivated olive tree, how much more will these who are the natural [branches] be grafted into their own olive tree? (Romans 11:17–18, 23-24)

So Gentiles, who did not originally receive the Law and Prophets, are united with Jewish brothers and sisters in God's covenant, which was promised in the Law and Prophets.

It is my prayer that, as we come to understand these truths, we will rethink the way we use "convert" and perhaps even remove it from our vocabulary, in joyful humility. Let us remember that none of us – Jewish or Gentile – can be united to God or each other without His compassionate work in our hearts!

Application

As either a Gentile or Jewish believer, how does your status as a "grafted-in" or "natural" branch affect your understanding of God's mercy and kindness?

Day 24

Advice for the Doctor

By this all people will know that you are My disciples: if you have love for one another.
John 13:35

It had been nearly two years since I had been to my physician in the United States (I spend most of my time overseas). I needed a routine check and blood test so I could continue to purchase my medication.

I looked around the familiar waiting room and smiled when I saw the familiar magazines (all in English) on the small side table. It seemed that nothing had changed in the office. I even recognized the nurse, who stepped out from an adjoining hallway and called my name, motioning me to follow.

In the examination room, I hiked myself up onto the crisp, white paper covering the padded table. The nurse asked a few preliminary questions while she took my blood pressure. She retrieved my medical file from a cabinet, inserted the newly recorded information, and said, "The doctor will be in to see you in a moment."

True to her word, the door soon opened. An unfamiliar face stepped into the room. Yes, he was a physician wearing a white medical coat and a stethoscope draped around his neck – but he was not my doctor.

Dr. Cohen introduced himself, greeting me warmly. I said hello in return, expressing my surprise at seeing this unexpected man.

After he looked through my file and asked some medical questions, Dr. Cohen said, "I see you're living out of the country. I also find that the name of the organization you work for begs a question."

I stiffened just a bit. When I first heard his name, I was quite certain my new physician was Jewish. I braced myself for a possibly difficult conversation. The name of Life in Messiah on my records left little doubt that I worked for a Christian agency with a Jewish-ministry emphasis.

Closing my file and looking me in the eye, Dr. Cohen challenged me, "So, do you tell Jewish people about Jesus? Is that what you do?" This was not really a question but more of a statement.

All of a sudden, the stiffness I had initially felt was gone. I calmly looked into his eyes and said, "Yes, that's exactly what I do, Dr. Cohen."

To my surprise, his face lit up and a wide smile filled his face. "Praise God!" he exclaimed. "I'm a born-again Jewish believer in Jesus!"

The next several minutes were wonderful as Dr. Cohen briefly told me how he had come to believe in Jesus. We talked about how grateful we both were to know the God of Abraham, Isaac, and Jacob. Our common faith and love for Israel provided an immediate bond.

Then the doctor asked me, the patient, "I would like your advice on something because of your familiarity with the faith and with the Jewish community."

"Sure, what is it?" I asked.

He explained that he and his wife were expecting their first child. As excited as he was, he was contemplating a perplexing matter: circumcision for his son.

I inquired what the issue was. Dr. Cohen responded, "Well, with both sets of our parents being Jewish, it's expected that we'll have our son circumcised. However, I don't want to do this because I'm no longer bound by the Law. It feels as if I'm being hypocritical or lacking faith if I have my son circumcised. What's your opinion?"

Almost instantly I told him, "If I were you, I would absolutely do it."

The doctor studied my face as I continued, "You already told me of the tension there is sometimes with your family. They already think you've turned your back on being Jewish because of your faith in Jesus. This is a terrific way to show them that you and your wife are still Jewish and you still love your heritage and culture.

It's also a way to show them that you know you're not bound by the Law (Romans 4:1–5:5), but justified by grace, through faith in Jesus (Ephesians 2:8–9). So, my advice would be to make your families happy; have your son circumcised. Celebrate it!"

Dr. Cohen asked, "You don't think it shows a lack of faith?"

"No," I responded. "I think it shows a loving faith, where you are considering the feelings of your family while knowing you are secure in your faith in the Messiah Jesus. That is an important thing. And perhaps walls will begin to break down so that, one day, they'll consider the truth of who Jesus is and what you and your wife have. By God's grace, perhaps they'll place their trust in Him for salvation, too!"

With this, the doctor looked at his patient and said, "That sounds like good advice."

Application

Whether you are Jewish or a "Goy with joy," celebrating our saving relationship with Messiah Jesus is a priority. We can both turn to God's Word to inform our decisions as we live out our faith in a multicultural world.

Day 25

An Unexpected Blessing

*He causes the grass to grow for the cattle,
And vegetation for the labor of mankind,
So that they may produce food from the earth,
And wine, which makes a human heart cheerful,
So that he makes his face gleam with oil,
And food, which sustains a human heart.
Psalm 104:14–15*

At Passover/Easter time each year I am reminded of a holiday dinner years ago when the "blessing" became a blessing. At the time, I was single and some good friends kindly extended an invitation to join them for lunch on Easter. My friends had known me for years. Over time, our relationship had changed, because I had changed! I had professed Jesus and placed my faith in Him a few years earlier and was not the same person they had been used to. They saw that my life was radically different; I really was a new person.

When I arrived at their home that Easter Sunday, I was not surprised – knowing how hospitable the couple had always been – when they introduced me to a stranger among the small group they had invited. As the young woman introduced herself as Rebecca, I felt certain she was Jewish. I thought to myself, *How awkward must she feel attending an Easter celebration as a Jewish woman!**

The air was filled with the aromatic scent of a smoked and spiced ham among all the other traditional foods attractively laid out on the dining table. As the family held an Easter egg hunt before lunch, I overheard them mentioning to the other guests that I had formerly been pretty "wild" but was now "religious" (Christian). After the hunt, everyone was seated, the ham was sliced, and beverages were served. It was quite festive! At this point the hosts decided it would only be fitting to ask me, their "religious" friend, to say a prayer before we partook of the feast.

Hesitating, I looked across the table at Rebecca, my new Jewish acquaintance. She certainly looked uncomfortable. I made a split-second decision. Rather than bowing my head, I lifted the glass and recited *Kiddush*, the traditional Hebrew blessing recited each Shabbat, followed with the Hebrew blessing for the Shabbat bread. Then I repeated both blessings in English.

**An Easter celebration, as a Christian holiday remembering a Messiah most Jewish people don't believe in and whom Jewish people have for centuries been wrongly accused of murdering, would be an uncomfortable experience for a Jewish nonbeliever.*

Everyone at the table looked a bit confused – except for Rebecca. Her tense, uncomfortable demeanor now lifted. She was much more relaxed as talk and laughter resumed, filling the room as various dishes of delicious food were passed around.

Later in the afternoon, the children went to play outside while the adults mingled and drank coffee. Rebecca approached me and simply said, "Thank you." She did not need to tell me what for. "You aren't Jewish, are you?" she asked.

I smiled and said, "No, but my Lord is" (Matthew 1:1–1:25; Isaiah 7:10–14, 9:6–7).

For the next few minutes, I was able to share with Rebecca about my faith and who Jesus is. I told her of my heart for Israel and the Jewish people because of the Messiah Jesus.

That evening, when I was back in my apartment, I thanked God that the Hebrew blessings I had recited had truly become a blessing, creating an opportunity to speak of the Holy One of Israel with one of the "lost sheep" of Israel.

Application

There is no greater message for Israel and Jewish communities than the message of salvation through the Messiah Jesus. What opportunities do you have to show God's love to the Jewish people around you?

Day 26

Grieving on Purpose

Pray for the peace of Jerusalem:
"May they prosper who love you."
Psalm 122:6

Yom HaShoah, Holocaust Remembrance Day, begins at sundown on the 27th day of Nisan on the Jewish calendar (it typically falls in April or May).

The Hebrew word *shoah* (שׁוֹאָה) is used 11 times in the *Tanakh* (Old Testament). It is translated into English as "waste, tempest, destruction, onslaught, devastation, or storm." Each word is an apt but inadequate descriptor of the carefully orchestrated, systematic murder of six million Jewish people by the Nazi party, who were often supported and abetted by the nations they conquered, between 1933 and 1945. Approximately 30% of Europe's Jewish population was destroyed in the Holocaust. In some cases, entire families and towns of extended families were annihilated.

Imagine six million losses. Calculate the impact of wiping out every living soul in Los Angeles and Chicago combined – or 222 cities the size of Life in Messiah's hometown of Lansing, Illinois.

Consider the impact on your family if one third of them (parents, siblings, grandparents, aunts, uncles, cousins) were killed during the 12-year period of the Holocaust. Remember, it's not just those killed during the *Shoah* (Holocaust) who are missing from your family, but also those who might have been born to them. How many branches of your tree would be missing or barren? Would you even be here?

Numbers alone are only a part of the grief; over the centuries, millions of people have been lost to war, famine, and ethnic cleansings. But the *Shoah's* systematic, science-supported, industrialized mass-destruction of Jewish people made it a new, grotesque phenomenon in the world, a lethal potion of human depravity and technical ingenuity.

The unmitigated hatred that fueled the *Shoah* is incomprehensible. Sociological factors of rage over a crumbling economy and political malfeasance cannot explain the murderous violence of the Nazis or ordinary citizens' just-as-deadly indifference toward their neighbors, co-workers, and friends who just happened to be Jewish. Even among those who proudly identified as Christians, few spoke up. Fewer still stood up to say "stop!" to the aggressors, or "let me help you" to the victims.

To my people, the *Shoah* is not just history; it is a living memory, shaping how we see ourselves in the world and reminding us of the ever-present, growing threat to our existence posed by antisemitism. We cannot process the current increase of anti-Jewish violence in places such as Brooklyn, New York; Paris, France; or Tel Aviv, Israel, without viewing it through the lens of the Shoah.

Understanding *Yom HaShoah* is essential for all who claim to love the Jewish people. To love the Jewish people without entering our grief casts doubt on the sincerity of that love, dimming the light of Messiah Yeshua's (Jesus') good news.

We at Life in Messiah encourage you to stand with the Jewish people in the commemoration of the Holocaust – not as an expression of personal guilt for past events in which you did not participate, or even out of grief for the church's past failures. Participate as a loving friend "grieving with those who grieve." Attend a commemoration service in a local synagogue, Jewish ministry on campus, Jewish community center, or online. Don't be shy about it – sympathetic Gentiles are welcome!

Above all, we encourage you to pray during *Yom HaShoah*; pray for God's beloved Jewish people and for believers who are serving among them. Pray for physical protection and wise responses as violent antisemitism rises globally. Pray for a spiritual awakening among the

Jewish people, that they will recognize in the *Shoah* the depth of human sin and everyone's need for God's forgiveness in Messiah. Pray for Life in Messiah's frontline workers, for wisdom in how to lovingly and patiently dismantle the cultural barriers to Jesus. Pray for Messiah's church around the world to take public, corporate, and practical stands against antisemitism, locally and internationally.

Thank you for standing with us and God's people. May Paul's words in Romans 9:1–5 resonate in our hearts:

> I am telling the truth in Christ, I am not lying; my conscience testifies with me in the Holy Spirit, that I have great sorrow and unceasing grief in my heart. For I could wish that I myself were accursed, separated from Christ for the sake of my countrymen, my kinsmen according to the flesh, who are Israelites, to whom belongs the adoption as sons and daughters, the glory, the covenants, the giving of the Law, the temple service, and the promises; whose are the fathers, and from whom is the Christ according to the flesh, who is over all, God blessed forever. Amen.

Application

What local event might you be able to attend during this year's *Yom HaShoah* to show your support for the Jewish people?

Day 27

Discovering Passover

And it shall be when your son asks you in time to come, saying, "What is this?" then you shall say to him, "With a powerful hand the LORD brought us out of Egypt, from the house of slavery."
Exodus 13:14

It was a chilly spring evening and a family member had invited my wife and me to attend a Passover meal. We had no idea what to expect. Neither of us had been to anything related to Passover before. We were curious to know why this particular church was hosting the event.

When we arrived at the church, we were directed into a dimly lit gymnasium. Our instruction pamphlets said there were several "stations" set up throughout the gymnasium, each one presenting an element associated with the story of the Israelite exodus out of Egypt.

I was surprised. I'd thought we were attending a sit-down Passover *meal*. I was hungry! Where was the food? *Oh, well*, I thought, *I will be out of here in an hour, and then I can grab some real food.*

In total silence (I would later learn the oddity of celebrating Passover in silence), we proceeded from station to station, learning each Passover seder element as we stopped at each table. This process continued until we reached the station for the *maror*, the bitter herbs that remind us of the bitterness of slavery.

By this point, I was very hungry. The instructions at the station said to take a small piece of unleavened bread (*matzah*), spread some bitter herbs on it, and eat it. Since I was hungry, I did what I thought any person would do: I loaded my *matzah* with bitter herbs until I could not fit any more. Then I proceeded to eat the whole thing in one big bite.

Until this point in my life, I do not recall having ever eaten spicy horseradish. I don't think my mom ever kept any in the house and I had never been offered any. If the horseradish had been labeled, I might not have attempted to satisfy my hunger with it. But alas, I experienced the reminder of "bitterness of bondage" in a very real way!

With eyes watering and sinuses instantly cleared, I no longer wanted any real food. Tears streamed down my cheeks as I searched for an escape from the bitterness. Unfortunately, no one had thought to set up any trash cans in the gym. I was helpless.

For some reason, I had virtually no knowledge of Passover when I attended my first Passover meal – despite having grown up in a church and holding a bachelor's degree in Christian education ministry. I had read the Exodus account of God's miraculous rescue and judgment against the gods of Egypt (Exodus 12:12), but I was unaware of Passover's significance throughout the Bible and continuing importance in today's Jewish community.

Of course, I was at fault for my ignorance. The Passover narrative (and other biblical feasts) had been right there in my Bible the whole time. Just because my church never taught about Passover did not excuse me for being ignorant of God's Word.

More than a decade has passed since that enlightening evening; I now understand that Passover is of great value to believers. Over the years I have studied Passover and led scores of Passover Seders; these studies have deepened my appreciation and understanding of God's Word, especially in the New Testament. I'd like to share some of my observations from the last 10 years.

First, the Passover sheds light on why the New Testament often refers to Jesus as a lamb. For example, John the Baptist called Jesus "the Lamb of God who takes away the sin of the world" (John 1:29). This was an intentional reference to the unblemished lambs the Israelites would select for sacrifice on the eve of

Passover (Exodus 12:3–6). John's Jewish listeners would have immediately grasped the pregnant meaning of Jesus' characterization as a lamb. The prophet Isaiah also referenced Passover, describing the Messiah as one "like a lamb that is led to slaughter" (Isaiah 53:7).

Second, the apostle Paul used Passover elements to teach biblical principles to believers. The Israelites were commanded to remove all leaven from their homes for Passover, the Feast of Unleavened Bread. If yeast was found in a family's home, they would be cut off from Israel (Exodus 12:19). Paul used that same principle to guide the church regarding unrepentant, immoral church members.

For example, Paul references the unleavened bread of Passover in 1 Corinthians 5:6–8, where he teaches on the harm caused by sin within the church:

> Your boasting is not good. Do you not know that a little leaven leavens the whole lump of dough? Clean out the old leaven so that you may be a new lump, just as you are in fact unleavened. For Christ our Passover also has been sacrificed. Therefore let's celebrate the feast, not with old leaven, nor with the leaven of malice and wickedness, but with the unleavened bread of sincerity and truth.

He uses the same Passover imagery in Galatians 5:9, writing, "A little leaven leavens the whole lump of dough."

Third, Paul referred to Jesus as "our Passover" (take another look at 1 Corinthians 5:7). In what way is Jesus our Passover?

At the first Passover, Israelites were commanded to select a perfect lamb, watching it for four days to ensure it was without blemish. Then, at twilight on the fourth day they were told to slaughter the perfect lamb. This task was not complete until each Israelite household had taken some of the blood and applied it to the doorposts and lintels of their homes. Only if the blood was applied to the door would the Lord "pass over" the home and not kill the firstborn male within (Exodus 12:23).

Just as lamb's blood had to be applied to save the lives of the firstborn males during the first Passover, so the blood of Jesus must be applied by faith to the doorposts and lintels of our hearts to save us from the bondage of sin and death (Romans 6:23).

These are just a few examples of how the New Testament uses Passover imagery. There is much more that could be said, including examples from the Old Testament, but I think I've made my point: learning about Passover provides a deeper appreciation and understanding of God's Word.

Application

Can you think of other Scripture passages that reference the Passover?

Day 28

A Divine Encounter

You who profess the LORD, take no rest for yourselves;
And give Him no rest
until He establishes
And makes Jerusalem an object of praise
on the earth.
Isaiah 62:6b–7

Recently a woman named Pauline asked if she could stop by Life in Messiah's home office. "I need help!" she said. Upon arrival, Pauline sat down with another staff member and me. Pauline delightedly told us about a chance encounter she'd had earlier that week.

A bit rushed, Pauline had chosen to grab lunch at a local fast-food place that she normally didn't frequent. As she entered, Pauline noticed a 30-something man hurrying across the wintry restaurant parking lot. Smiling, she held the door open for him. He thanked her and they joined the line at the register, engaging in easy conversation.

Pauline showed genuine interest and kindness toward the young man – so much so that he invited her to join him at a table so they could continue their chat. When they sat to eat, he introduced himself as Frank. Then he asked Pauline if she'd like to pray for the meal. He correctly assumed she was a Christian!

The two had a great conversation over lunch. Frank readily told Pauline about his Jewish upbringing. Like many in his generation, Frank described himself as "religiously nonobservant," even though his grandfather and father were active in synagogue. Frank had married a Gentile girl; they weren't attending services anywhere. "But I believe in God," he stated.

As they finished lunch and parted ways, Frank readily gave his contact info for further communication. That's what had brought Pauline to us.

"Where do I go from here?" Pauline asked us. "I have a strong sense that there was a purpose in our meeting."

We agreed with Pauline: the meeting had clearly been divinely orchestrated, not by chance. She'd already taken the important first step by representing the Lord in a loving way to Frank. He hadn't been turned off by Pauline's identity as a follower of Jesus. Indeed, he'd seemed intrigued to know more, especially when she'd spoken of her love for the Jewish people.

The three of us talked for an hour, offering guidance for Pauline's next steps.

"There's no substitute for being controlled by the Holy Spirit," we told her. Just as the Lord arranged for Pauline's and Frank's paths to cross and for Frank to want to continue the discussion, He also had a plan for the future. "Pray for wisdom and trust Him to guide you!" we told Pauline. "Saving souls is God's job; we're just His messengers."

We also suggested, "If Frank indeed wants to get together, find a time and place to meet. Perhaps his wife, who comes from a Christian background, will want to join the conversation."

We advised Pauline to ask clarifying questions to ascertain where Frank and his wife were spiritually and what their questions and perceived needs were. We pointed out, "You said Frank has already alluded to the challenge of raising kids in this world with its evils. As a mom of grown kids, you have much to share of how the Lord helped you parent!"

We encouraged Pauline that she had already shown adeptness for recognizing conversational bridges to spiritual matters. "Be prepared to share the gospel, preferably from a perspective Frank can relate to," we advised. "Even secular Jews have a strong sense of Jewish identity. Since Messiah was promised to Israel first, we have the tremendous advantage of pointing to the Hebrew prophets and how God revealed to them the identity of the Promised One."

We assured Pauline that we would continue to be an available resource and that we did not consider her visit a distraction from our office work. Equipping believers to share their faith with Jewish friends has been a central purpose of Life in Messiah since our founding in 1887.

Before we parted, we lifted Pauline up in prayer, asking God for His wisdom and empowerment. We also prayed for Frank and his family, asking the Spirit to prepare their hearts to hear and receive the Good News.

If Pauline had been energetic when she'd first arrived, she was positively enthusiastic when she left, taking an armful of evangelistic literature with her. She couldn't wait to improve on her acquaintance with Frank and his wife.

Application

How eager are you to testify of God's saving grace in your life? Are you prepared to share your faith when opportunities arise? We hope this book has been helpful as you consider how to share your hope with others.

Day 29

The Slippery Slope of Spiritual Merit

Therefore, if you have been raised with Christ, keep seeking the things that are above, where Christ is, seated at the right hand of God. Set your minds on the things that are above, not on the things that are on earth.
Colossians 3:1–2

Live music caught our attention as my Life in Messiah colleague and I stepped out of the convention center in downtown Vancouver. Looking across the open square, we saw a large group, ranging from children to middle-aged adults, performing a folk dance.

Curious, we approached their booth, where a man and woman quickly engaged us in conversation. Within 30 seconds, my colleague and I knew we were talking to members of a cult. They explained what their group was all about, citing Acts 2:44: "And all believers were together and had all things in common; and they would sell their property and possessions and share them with all, to the extent that anyone had need." They beamed as they described their way of life.

"I live in a house with 50 other people," the man said proudly. "We live like the early church, sharing all things in common."

"We're learning to love each other and not be selfish," the woman added with a gentle smile.

They explained how they'd found all the answers in this community, how if only they'd known sooner, they wouldn't have lost their children to the world; how wonderful life was now that they were living it God's way. Unlike the fallen institution known as the church, their community was truly embodying what God had always meant the church to be.

We listened, feeling trapped, knowing we could say nothing to help them. From their perspective we were outsiders – fallen and deceived people who needed the answers they were offering. When we spoke, the world spoke through us, and this community had left the things of the world behind.

Eventually my colleague graciously excused us and we resumed our original goal of finding a place for lunch.

The encounter left me pondering how an idea straight from the Bible could be used to create something so wrong. Can anyone who starts with biblical principles end up in the same place? If so, how can I – and other believers – avoid making the same mistake?

As I researched the cult over the following weeks, what stuck out to me was their interpretation of Acts 2:44

as an imperative – as the verse to interpret all others, the principle delineating the faithful from the fallen. More than Scripture as a whole, Acts 2:44 had become the group's compass. And somewhere in the process, they'd lost sight of the gospel.

As an organization, Life in Messiah exists to reach the Jewish people with the gospel and to equip the church to do the same. Our message? That God loves and desires a personal relationship with each individual, and this relationship can only happen through Jesus (John 14:6). Our focus? We want everyone to hear the gospel, but we have a special burden for the Jewish people.

All believers, including those involved in Jewish ministry, must regularly examine our hearts to ensure the gospel remains foremost. Jesus needs to be the center of our daily lives, our spiritual lives, our ministry, our theology, and our motives.

There is benefit in understanding and appreciating Jewish thought, values, and traditions; this understanding is key to communicating the gospel with sensitivity. However, we must be vigilant not to lose sight of Messiah in our love for His people.

As concrete beings living in a concrete world, we crave certainty. This human trait makes us vulnerable to a particular brand of deception that legalism, the Prosperity Gospel, and religious cults all share. Each of these iterations presents faith as a divine recipe, offering a list of ingredients and step-by-step instructions that, carefully followed, will yield the desired benefit: health and wealth, God-fearing children, moral purity, etc.

Some of us are drawn to the reverence and structure of Jewish culture, which is steeped in ancient tradition. Indeed, celebrating Passover, observing Shabbat, or attending a Messianic congregation may impart spiritual benefit, enriching our understanding of Scripture and the context it was written in.

However, we must not conflate spiritual benefit with spiritual merit. Being Jewish or connected with Jewish culture or customs does not earn us extra favor with God. Referring to God by His Hebrew name does not make us closer to Him. Jewish believers are not somehow more saved than Gentile believers; we are all saved by the blood of Messiah. Each of these good things is subordinate to God Himself.

God made it clear to Moses that making Israel His chosen people was an act of grace. God told Moses,

> The Lord did not make you His beloved nor choose you because you were greater in number than any of the peoples, since you were the fewest of all peoples, but because the Lord loved you and kept the oath which He swore to your forefathers, the Lord brought you out by a mighty hand and redeemed you from the house of slavery, from the hand of Pharaoh king of Egypt. Know therefore that the Lord your God, He is God, the faithful God,

who keeps His covenant and His faithfulness to a thousand generations for those who love Him and keep His commandments. (Deuteronomy 7:6–16)

The focus of this passage isn't on who God's chosen people are, but on who God is: He is loving, He is faithful, He keeps His promises to a thousand generations!

God did not choose the Jewish people because they are special; they are special because He chose them. Just as Gentile believers are chosen by Him. "Therefore, as you have received Christ Jesus the Lord, so walk in Him, having been firmly rooted and now being built up in Him and established in your faith" (Colossians 2:6–7).

In Colossians 2, Paul makes it clear that keeping Jesus the center of our lives and beliefs is vital to our faith. He warns us not to be taken captive by philosophy, deception, human tradition (Colossians 2:8), customs regarding food and drink, festivals, the Sabbath (Colossians 2:16–17), decrees, self-made religion, or asceticism, which are "of no value against fleshly indulgence" (Colossians 2:20–23). Rather, Paul passionately urges his readers to "[hold] firmly to the head, from whom the entire body, being supplied and held together by the joints and ligaments, grows with a growth which is from God" (Colossians 2:19).

Anything – good or bad – that supplants the Messiah in our lives is a danger to our souls. As soon as our eyes stray from the gospel in favor of another good thing, that good thing becomes a trap.

Therefore, if you have been raised with Christ, keep seeking the things that are above, where Christ is, seated at the right hand of God. Set your minds on the things that are above, not on the things that are on earth. For you have died, and your life is hidden with Christ in God. When Christ, who is our life, is revealed, then you also will be revealed with Him in glory. (Colossians 3:1–4)

Application

Read Colossians 2 in full. If *Sharing God's Heart* has encouraged you to learn more about Jewish ministry, we rejoice! But it is vital that our interest in a culture, tradition, or people not supplant the gospel's place in our hearts. Ask God to maintain in you a gospel-centered love for the Jewish people.

Day 30

Why Jewish Ministry?

For I am not ashamed of the gospel, for it is the power of God for salvation to everyone who believes, to the Jew first and also to the Greek.
Romans 1:16

Jewish ministry is not an easy calling: barriers to the gospel are abundant and professions of faith are few. Many ask why we would devote ourselves to Jewish ministry, when there are so many other people groups who need the gospel – and who are more open to receiving it.

The short answer is that Jewish ministry is important because the Jewish people are important to God. We see this demonstrated in Scripture in two primary ways: in the origins of the Messiah, and the biblical emphasis on God's heart for the Jewish people.

Romans 9:4–5 sums up the first point well: "To [Israel] belongs the adoption as sons and daughters, the glory, the covenants, the giving of the Law, the temple service, and the promises; whose are the fathers, and from whom is the Christ according to the flesh, who is over all, God blessed forever. Amen."

Jesus the Messiah came to us in the flesh as a Jewish man, descended through His mother, Mary, from a long line of Jewish men and women. Our Savior's genealogy traces back to Abraham, to whom God first made a promise to bless all the nations through Abraham's descendants (Genesis 12:3). Not only was Jesus a Jewish man, His earthly ministry was first and foremost to other Jewish people. He told the Canaanite woman, "I was sent only to the lost sheep of the house of Israel" (Matthew 15:24).

After Jesus' ascension, the gospel spread to the Gentile world through His Jewish disciples' efforts, particularly through Paul (the book of Acts details Paul's conversion and subsequent ministry). The early church was a Jewish phenomenon – so much so that its Jewish leaders called a special council to determine how Gentiles who were coming to faith should fit into the church (Acts 15).

It is true that Israel as a whole has never embraced Jesus as their Messiah. As Paul says, "But by their wrongdoing salvation has come to the Gentiles, to make [Israel] jealous" (Romans 11:11). Paul points out that, if the world was blessed through Israel's hardening, the blessing will be even greater when Israel at last turns back to God (verse 12)!

This brings us to the second point drawing us to Jewish ministry: the biblical emphasis on God's love and calling for the Jewish people and their eventual restoration.

Romans 1:16 is just one of many passages that place a special emphasis on Jewish salvation. Paul, who devoted his ministry to preaching the gospel to Gentiles, always appealed first to the Jewish inhabitants wherever he traveled. He had a deep passion to see his Jewish brothers bow the knee to the Messiah (Romans 9:1–3).

Romans 10:1, a prayer for the Jewish people, is the only instance of prayer for a specific people group's salvation! This is not to say that Jewish people are more important than other people groups, but it does reveal the prominence of Israel – and Jerusalem – in God's plans for the world.

This prominence is prevalent, of course, throughout the Old Testament. In Genesis 12:3, God promises that those who bless the Jewish people will themselves be blessed and the one who curses them will be cursed (Genesis 12:3). Psalm 122:6 calls its readers to pray for the peace of Jerusalem, and Isaiah writes, "You who profess the LORD, take no rest for yourselves; and give Him no rest until He establishes and makes Jerusalem an object of praise on earth" (Isaiah 62:6b–7).

This theme of a longed-for redemption of Israel and Jerusalem continues in the New Testament. Jesus Himself said,

> Jerusalem, Jerusalem, the city that kills the prophets and stones those who have been sent to her! How

often I wanted to gather your children together, just as a hen gathers her young under her wings, and you were unwilling! Behold, your house is left to you desolate; and I say to you, you will not see Me until you say, "Blessed is the One who comes in the name of the Lord!" (Luke 13:34–35)

Nowhere in these impassioned cries do we get the impression that Israel's rejection of Jesus and His messengers invalidates God's covenant with the Jewish people. In Romans 11:25–32, Paul emphasizes that God's promises and plans for Israel still stand, "for the gifts and the calling of God are irrevocable" (Romans 11:29).

Scripture is clear that God has loved the Jewish people in the past and has promised their repentance in the future. Let us not forget that God also loves the Jewish people in the times between. There are thousands of Jewish people living *now* who need to hear the Good News. There are countless individuals whom God is preparing to recognize Jesus as the long-awaited Jewish Messiah – and often He uses believers like you and me to plant the seeds of the gospel in Jewish hearts.

When Jesus ascended into heaven after His earthly ministry, He left the church this command: "Go, therefore, and make disciples of all the nations, baptizing them in the name of the Father and the Son and the Holy Spirit, teaching them to follow all that I commanded you; and behold, I am with you always, to the end of the age" (Matthew 28:19–20).

The events of history have caused the Jewish people to be scattered through countless nations across the earth. As we, the church, go into all the nations to baptize and teach, let us not neglect the Jewish people within those nations!

Application

Is God prompting you to reach out to a Jewish family member, friend, neighbor, or coworker? Do you sense a call to Jewish ministry? Or are you simply curious about Life in Messiah? We encourage you to visit our website, lifeinmessiah.org, to learn more.

KEEP LEARNING

To learn more about Jewish evangelism, Jewish culture and history, or standing against antisemitism, visit www.lifeinmessiah.org/resources. There you will find curated lists of websites, books, and films to help you dive deeper into these important topics.

You can also scan the QR code below to access this resource.

If this book has been an encouragement to you, please pass it on to someone else or consider making a donation at www.lifeinmessiah.org/donate.

Made in the USA
Monee, IL
08 August 2024